Praise for *Locked Up*

This remarkable prison memoir reveals the heart of a political dissenter and the soul of a Christian believer. *Locked Up* gives witness to real-life conditions inside an American cell block—the arbitrary rules; the climate of fear, frustration, and brokenness. It comes from the hand of an exceptional individual who is alive to moments of reconciliation and beauty even as he ponders the contradictions between gospel power and imperial power. Don Beisswenger is probing, watchful, hopeful, unafraid to face doubts—above all, a man in love with God's world.

—RAY WADDLE
Columnist, editor of *Reflections* magazine, and
author of *Against the Grain: Unconventional Wisdom from Ecclesiastes*

In a world torn by war, violence, and poverty, we need more people like Don Beisswenger. As a person of deep faith, Don has taught us by example that action is an integral part of our faith journey. Don is a true peacemaker, and his life and book will touch you deeply.

—FATHER ROY BOURGEOIS
Founder, SOA Watch
Columbus, Georgia

I was deeply touched by Don's recounting of his experiences in prison. He has a very good way of portraying his situation, feelings, periods of uneasiness, and relationships with others. *Locked Up* has a directness that conveys authenticity, not self-consciousness. It is a winsome and powerful witness.

—DR. JAMES T. LANEY
Former ambassador to South Korea
President emeritus, Emory University

This memoir grabs you by the heartstrings and refuses to let go. Moving with Don Beisswenger from protest to prison, we come to appreciate his deep commitment to stop the violence toward our sisters and brothers in Latin America and around the world. From the moment of his incarceration until his release, we experience the tragedy of prison life. His was a crime of passion—a passion for justice, peace, and love. We should all be so convicted!

—REV. JUDI HOFFMAN
Pastor, Edgehill United Methodist Church
Nashville, Tennessee

When we visited Don Beisswenger at the federal prison in Kentucky where he was serving his sentence for civil disobedience, he told us he was keeping a journal. This is it—the memoir of a prisoner of conscience who wrote his way to freedom. In these pages Don offers impressive proof that he was, quite literally, saved by the pen.

—WILL CAMPBELL AND JOHN EGERTON
Authors living in the Nashville, Tennessee, area

This touching and thoughtful book posits the question, what does it mean to be a Christian prisoner of conscience in contemporary America? Readers of this book will be moved to personal reflection and examination regarding their own personal witness. *Locked Up* impressed me as a thoughtful, sensitive work by a true disciple.

—FRANK E. DOBSON JR.
Director, Bishop Joseph Johnson Black Cultural Center
Vanderbilt University

Locked Up plummets you into the world of prisons, where hundreds of hidden rules exist to punish or demean, boring days pass picking up trash, and nights are disrupted by 3:00 a.m. head counts. Prophet and protester Beisswenger weaves his passion for justice, his cell-block view of prison life, his struggle to survive, and his life of faith into an absorbing and challenging tale.

—LARRY J. PEACOCK
Author of *Openings, A Daybook of Saints, Psalms, and Prayer*
Director of Rolling Ridge Retreat Center, North Andover, Massachusetts

Don Beisswenger's imprisonment for protests against a brutal and inhumane institution was his first gift to our country, our churches, and us. His second gift was to write about his first gift: insightfully, resolutely, compassionately, reflectively, and always in hope. Such gifts can only stir in us our very deepest gratitude.

—EDWARD FARLEY
Author of *Practicing Gospel: Unconventional Thoughts on the Church's Ministry*
Professor emeritus, Vanderbilt University Divinity School

Locked Up gives us an account of a man who serves time willingly for an act of civil disobedience. The story of that action and his subsequent imprisonment poses an interesting question for all of us. As Reinhold Niebuhr put it, Don is either a "fool for Christ" or "a damn fool." This book enables us to determine what kind of fool Don Beisswenger is and to ask ourselves, are we willing to be fools for the sake of Christ?

—REV. JOSEPH B. INGLE
United Church of Christ minister and pastor to the condemned

LOCKED UP

Letters *and* Papers *of a*
Prisoner *of* Conscience

Don Beisswenger

UPPER
ROOM BOOKS®
NASHVILLE

LIBRARY OF CONGRESS CATALOGING-IN-PUBLICATION DATA
Beisswenger, Donald F.
Locked up : letters and papers of a prisoner of conscience / Don Beisswenger.
    p. cm.
Includes bibliographical references.
ISBN 978-0-8358-9939-0
    1. Beisswenger, Donald F. 2. Presbyterian Church (U.S.A.)—Clergy—Biography.
3. Political prisoners—United States—Biography. 4. U.S. Army School of the Americas.
I. Title.
BX9225.B348A3 2007
285′.1092—dc22
[B]
                                                                    2007029992
Printed in the United States of America

Dedicated with appreciation to
three women who have shaped my life:
Julie, Joyce, Judy

And to Harmon L. Wray (1947–2007),
treasured friend, valued colleague,
witness to God's reign among us in word and deed

CONTENTS

ACKNOWLEDGMENTS

I give testimony to those who helped move this writing from inchoate thoughts in my mind into more intelligible statements. I thank Judy (Pilgrim) Bcisswenger for her translation of my scrawl into first drafts. Her diligence was remarkable. Many people encouraged me as I prepared the material for larger circulation; I am grateful for Martha and Hoyt Hickman, John Egerton, Will Campbell, Ed Farley, Harmon Wray, and Bill Barnes. Victor Judge did a superb work in preparing material for publication in Vanderbilt University Divinity School's *The Spire*. I express deep appreciation to Anne Crumpler, who did major work on the initial editing of the material I wrote while in prison. What a gift she was! Kathleen Stephens and Anne Trudel provided the final editing and compiling of photos and other materials. They were a joy to work with. Thank you. To all these I express deep appreciation.

Several groups of people in Nashville and around the country provided support both during the time I made my witness and the subsequent time I spent in prison. I note each of them with appreciation: Presbyterian Peace Fellowship, Edgehill United Methodist Church, Hillsboro Presbyterian Church, Vanderbilt Divinity School, The Open Door Community, Nashville Peace and Justice Center, La Casa, Penuel Ridge Contemplative Retreat Center, Witness for Peace, the Interdenominational Ministers' Fellowship, and the staff of the School of the Americas Watch.

Thanks to the following people who visited me in prison: Judy Pilgrim; Steve Monhollen; Bill Barnes; John Egerton; Will Campbell; Matt Leber; David and Pam Kidd; Tom, Mary, and Sara Beisswenger; Kathryn Mitchum; Philip, Bacilia, Daniel, and Matthew Beisswenger; Linda and Jim Zralek; Mitzi and John Wolf; Roger Golden; Lee Limbird; Carol Freund; Ron Turner; Kathy Masulis; Bill and Margaret Howell; Erik Johnson; Jim and Berta Laney; Eugene and Penny TeSelle; Janet Wolf; Drew Beisswenger; and Suzanne, Jim,

Emily, and Parker Ross. Two persons wanted to visit but were not given permission: Harmon Wray and Cinny Poppin.

The inmates at Manchester Prison became a major part of my support group while I was incarcerated, for which I am grateful. My children and grandchildren were a community of support for me as well.

Finally, I am grateful to the Living Room, a weekly gathering of homeless persons and friends who listen to one another. During my time in prison, they placed an empty chair in the circle each week to include me in their fellowship. John, Jerry, Doris, and Judy all played a role in this drama and miracle of love.

soli Deo gratia

PREFACE

From April 6, 2004, until October 1, 2004, I was incarcerated in the federal prison located in Manchester, Kentucky. In protesting the School of the Americas (SOA), now called the Western Hemisphere Institute for Security Cooperation (WHINSEC) [see Appendix A], I crossed the barrier onto the U.S. Army base at Fort Benning, Georgia, and was charged with criminal trespass. Standing before Judge G. Mallon Faircloth of the U.S. District Court in Columbus, Georgia, I pleaded guilty to charges of taking six steps past a No Trespassing sign. For my act of civil disobedience, I was arrested, charged, tried, convicted, fined $1,000, and sentenced to six months in prison.

Solitude, meditation, and prayer helped me to survive in confinement. Writing down my thoughts helped me to clarify what was going on within and around me and to discern how I could respond appropriately and faithfully. As I wrote, I often reflected on what God seemed to be inviting me to be—both internally and in the common life of the prison.

My papers from prison are diverse. I wrote letters to about two hundred people who wanted to keep in touch with me. It was a privilege to belong to a community of caring people! I also kept a journal (written in address books because prison authorities returned the blank journals sent to me), in which I reflected on various aspects of my life in prison, the people I met, and the problems I faced. I wanted to tell what I found out about myself, others, and the world. Finally, I also received poems, letters, and cartoons from many of my correspondents. They added to my life, and I was grateful for them.

As I read over these papers, three themes emerged. First was my awareness early on that to survive I would need to keep in touch with my life in the Spirit. The interior aspects of Christian faith have been a vital part of my life. I have learned how to be alone, to engage God in solitude as well as in public worship and study. Martin Luther described the nature of Christian faith as living before God. Reflections on my life before God are woven through and define the content of this book.

I entered prison on the third day of Holy Week; I was keenly aware of Jesus' arrest and incarceration, an arrest that ended in execution. I considered the meaning of the Lord's Supper in a prison context and reflected on the laundry room as a place for daily prayer and meditation. Throughout my time in prison, I continually sought to discern my calling. I originally thought that I would lead a Bible study, but I was not permitted to do so. So what was I called to do? I asked a number of other inmates what they saw as their goal in prison. To a person, they said survival. My interior life, my life in the Spirit, became essential for survival, for keeping me human and alive before God.

Second, I have described aspects of life in prison. The physical aspects of prison are limited to my cubicle, the garden, the recreation areas, the room where we ate, and the exercise barn. There is a geography to faith. We see things differently when we are with new people in strange situations.

> AT FIRST I WAS PERPLEXED ABOUT BEING IN PRISON . . . . LATER I REFLECTED ON CONFINEMENT AS A GIFT.

At first I was perplexed about being in prison. While confined, I was disrespected, demeaned, mistreated, and berated. Later I reflected on confinement as a gift. I kept in my mind and heart the people of Latin America who had been victims of the SOA. Their murder and torture had led to my resistance, and remembering them kept me alive to God's call to be a voice for the abused and oppressed.

The third theme describes how my life in prison was connected to life outside of prison. People visited each week. My relationship with Judy Pilgrim blossomed, and her letters empowered me. I wrote letters to my six children and their families. Friends wrote and visited almost every week; each was an agent of God's Spirit. The correspondence I received from people around the nation, even the world, was a sign to me of God's love. One letter written by a seventeen-year-old girl from Berwyn, Illinois, was especially moving.

To help me remember the atrocities committed by SOA/WHINSEC, I posted on my bulletin board a picture of Dorothy Kazel, one of the missionaries raped and murdered by SOA-trained death squads. I continued my interest in the SOA Watch and in efforts to close the school. I reflected on the increasing cost of dissent in our nation.

JOYCE PERKINS

These three themes are woven throughout the material that follows, which proceeds month by month through my time in prison. Entering prison had a peculiar power, but so did leaving. In both cases, I was grateful for the people who shared the moment with me.

In the end, I found my calling: to be a human being in my relationships and in my witness. I learned to attend to beauty as well as to cruelty and inhumanity. I discovered that I am also called to help others respond to the realities of prison life and seek reconciling justice in our society.

I hope that reading this book will strengthen you in your life before God—as a person and in your concern for all those social, economic, political, and cultural structures that God intends to be righteous and just.

A CHRONOLOGY OF EVENTS

1996 Don Beisswenger retires from Vanderbilt University Divinity School as professor of church and community; is named professor emeritus; begins to work more vigorously to resist the global war against the poor; works with the homeless in Nashville; and continues studies and engagement with the poor of Latin America, an interest that developed in 1980 with the murder of Oscar Romero and the rapes and murders of four missionaries

1997 participates in first vigil at Fort Benning, Georgia

1999 participates in second vigil at Fort Benning and crosses the line with over two thousand other people; is arrested and given a five-year ban and issued a bar letter

2002 participates in third vigil; crosses the line again; violates (inadvertently) the five-year ban and terms of the bar letter; twenty-seven persons are arrested and taken to the Fort Benning armory; they are searched, finger-printed, and secured with chains around their arms and legs before being taken to the Muscogee County Jail for thirty-six hours; the judge arraigns Beisswenger and sets bail at $1,000; bail previously had been set at $500

2004

stands trial with other defendants on January 26 and is sentenced to six months in federal prison; fined $1,000; will not receive Social Security payments while in prison; other defendants are sentenced to six months, three months, a fine, or probation

reports to prison in Manchester, Kentucky, on April 6; turns over garments but is permitted to keep eyeglasses and two Bibles

is released from prison on October 1 and returns to Nashville for a reception at the Peace and Justice Center

delivers first reflections on confinement during a service at the Downtown Presbyterian Church in Nashville

participates in fourth vigil at Fort Benning; does not cross the line

2005

begins organizing correspondence and journal entries from the period of confinement

What creeps into
my mind
is the little fear,
or big,
that when it
touches me
very personally,
will I be faithful?
—Maura Clark

Sister Maura Clark was a Maryknoll Sister who, along with Sister Ita Ford, Lay Missioner Jean Donovan, and Ursuline Sister Dorothy Kazel, were murdered in El Salvador in 1980.

[1]
FROM PROTEST TO PRISON

Christian faith in salvation and liberation is based on a fundamental conviction that nothing in the world is simply fated to be. There is nothing in the universe that simply cannot be helped. No evil is so impregnable as to be absolutely irremediable. Everything is capable of renewal, and the world is destined to realize the utopia of the reign of God.

—LEONARDO BOFF

After my wife, Joyce, died in December 2002, I grieved, acknowledging the loss of my partner of fifty years. Dealing with this new reality in my life was a slow yet wondrous process. I decided that I did not want to be called "widower" and instead came up with the term "husband emeritus." Joyce has a permanent place in my life and in my heart, but once she was gone, I had the freedom to act upon my beliefs in a way I had not had before.

I chose to become more involved in protesting U.S. foreign policy in Latin America. While I had studied the situation for more than twenty years and had traveled throughout most of Latin America in the course of eight visits, now I considered engaging in acts of civil disobedience. I reflected on what Martin Luther King Jr. said after reading Henry David Thoreau's essay "On Civil Disobedience"—that noncooperation with evil is as much a moral obligation as is cooperation with good. I was about to act on King's wisdom.

Sunday, November 23, 2003

Along with twenty-six others, I crossed onto the army base at Fort Benning, Georgia. Our vigil had begun with the reading of names of victims of disappearances, torture, and murder by graduates of SOA/WHINSEC.

Our affinity group of nine people and a group of supporters moved up a hill north of the main entrance to Fort Benning and walked down a closed street with concrete abutments at the end. After September 11, 2001, a fence was constructed to prevent people from walking onto the base, so we jumped over it.

Marching in the funeral vigil procession before my arrest

Immediately I was arrested and told to kneel down. Having some experience with kneeling, I obeyed and even said a prayer. The arresting officer handcuffed my hands behind my back. The others knelt and were also handcuffed. All of us were taken by bus to a large building, where we were frisked. There we were fingerprinted and had chains put around our ankles and torsos as well as our hands. We walked in chains to the bus and were taken to the Muscogee County Jail, where we were held for thirty-six hours.

One of our group, a classics professor who was blind, was released, and the remaining thirteen men and thirteen women were split up into different sections of the jail. In the men's section, there were several tables ringed by rooms with metal beds and a toilet. As we waited for our supper of soup, bread, and fruit, another protester, a Jesuit priest, and I talked about our lives as teachers.

Twenty-four of the twenty-seven defendants in the January 2004 School of the Americas Watch trials in Columbus, Georgia. I am on the back row, fourth from left.

Monday, November 24

This morning, each of us was called to court to be arraigned. The judge asked the prosecuting attorney the nature of our transgressions and then set the amount of our bail. Our lawyer argued that I should be released on my own recognizance. The judge promptly set the bond at $1,000, twice the amount of bail the year before. Evidently, the cost of dissent has gone up.

In the courtroom were many friends, including Len Bjorkman, chair of the Presbyterian Peace Fellowship, who proved to be a rich source of counsel and care. Presbyterian Peace Fellowship members had given me their blessing before my arrest, and Lois, one of their members, donated money for my bail.

Tonight I stayed at the Open Door in Atlanta, a ministry for the homeless. The people at Open Door have stood with me through the years and now offered their support.

Tuesday, November 25

I left for Nashville this morning, feeling tired but ready for the next steps in my journey.

Monday, January 26, 2004

Eight weeks after our arrest, all twenty-six of us who were arrested appeared in Judge G. Mallon Faircloth's court in Columbus, Georgia. With the others who would plead guilty I sat along the wall under a sign containing a quotation by Jimmy Carter about justice in the land. A number of people in the courtroom were there to support me. Among them were Carrie and Abby, from Nashville; Tex Thomas, representing the Interdenominational Ministers' Fellowship; my friend Judy Pilgrim; and my son Tom.

> As THE REALITY OF MY SENTENCE SET IN, I WONDERED HOW I WOULD STAY ALIVE WHILE IN PRISON.

With Tom standing beside me, I stated my case to the judge [see Appendix B]. My lawyer then sought to have the case dismissed, based on my age (seventy-three) and character. Judge Faircloth paused, then accepted my guilty plea to the charge of criminal trespass. He sentenced me to six months in prison and fined me $1,000. I knew I would lose my Social Security benefits while in prison.

As the reality of my sentence set in, I wondered how I would stay alive while in prison. How would I keep in touch with people? What should I bring?

Upon returning to Nashville, I gathered a group of about twenty people to support me and to keep alive the work of closing the SOA/WHINSEC.

Sunday, March 14

A portion of a letter to friends and family regarding the reasons for my dissent

Dietrich Bonhoeffer said, "Let him who cannot be alone beware of community." He also said, "Let him who is not in community beware of being alone."[1] This letter expresses my joy in a community that sustained me during the stress and difficulties prior to the trial.

What joy I felt when we gathered at my home to discuss SOA/WHINSEC and your support for my small witness!

It has become clear to me that U.S. foreign policy in Latin America reveals the broader dimensions of our nation's militaristic policies. Central to those policies are the economic interests of the United States and the maintenance of our security and lifestyle without regard for the poor and the earth itself. Our military policies reveal the "arrogance of power," about which Senator J. William Fulbright spoke in his book of the same title.[2]

Militarism is a central issue, seen clearly as military prowess is juxtaposed with children, mothers, and sweatshop workers. We are on the side of the wealthy, the powerful, and the violent.

> February 26, 2004
>
> Dear Don-the pride of Nashville,
>
> As I recall, you are about to start your six months in jail. I have the impression you will get along well with your fellow inmates, who will appreciate your pastoral touch. . . .
>
> If you write from jail, I'll be sure to answer.
>
> Most affectionately, dear Don,
>
> *Bill*
>
> William Sloane Coffin

Saturday, April 3

I spent the past two days in retreat at Penuel Ridge, a retreat center that a group of us started in Nashville twenty years ago. Cinny Poppin and Roger Golden led a moving liturgy each morning and afternoon. Then a community send-off was held at St. Ann's Episcopal Church in east Nashville. A bright spring day greeted those who gathered for a service of song, prayer, and

My grandchildren join me in leading a procession to the Federal Building. L to R: Rachel Hellewell, Sara Beisswenger, me, Daniel Beisswenger, and Dylan Hellewell.

reflection, led by various friends and colleagues. My son Tom spoke of his delight in being there, of his pride in my action, and of his fear and uncertainty about my future. The group gathered in a circle to lay hands on me and pray. I sat in the middle of the circle with my grandson Matthew on my lap. My son Philip offered a prayer. Joy and gladness mingled with my apprehension, uncertainty, fear, and panic.

The group then walked together to the Federal Building, about a mile away. Four of my grandchildren—Daniel, Sara, Dylan, and Rachel—joined me in leading the procession.

The participants moved single file down the street, carrying mock caskets and crosses. One person called out the names of people who had been brutalized or murdered by graduates of SOA/WHINSEC. As the names were read, the people shouted, "*Presente!*" ("Present!"). A rally at the courthouse concluded my send-off. I felt honored to be part of an awesome event and grateful for those who had planned it as a testimony to our city.

Judy Pilgrim and my grandson Dylan in front of the Federal Building in Nashville

—⁂—

I received word early this month that I should report April 6 to the federal prison in Manchester, Kentucky. Later I learned that I could bring nothing except a Bible, my eyeglasses, and my watch. I was concerned about whether I could bring my medicines for diabetes.

A MAN OF PEACE, AT AGE 73, PAYS RIDICULOUS PRICE
by Will D. Campbell

When a nation becomes so insecure that it sends elderly and ill citizens to prison for taking a few steps on native ground, that nation is in danger of losing its soul. Or so it seems to me.

I am referring to an aging prophet named Don Beisswenger, 73, a Nashvillian who has been sentenced to half a year in federal prison and fined a thousand dollars for taking six steps past a NO TRESPASSING sign at Fort Benning, Ga.

I could call the Rev. Beisswenger good and righteous and . . . all those adjectives apply. But a better designation is the strong noun *prophet*: one who teaches and lives by biblical authority. However we describe him, he is a man of faith and good deeds.

I have known Don Beisswenger for 40 years. This modest and unassuming man has demonstrated—through his teaching in the Divinity School at Vanderbilt University, his ministry to the homeless in Nashville and Atlanta and Chicago, his realized vision for the highly respected Penuel Ridge Retreat Center, and his devotion to his wife and life partner, Joyce, so recently departed—that he is a virtuous human being.

But he took six harmless steps over an arbitrary line to bear witness against the teachings of the School of the Americas/Western Hemisphere Institute for Security Cooperation (SOA/WHISC) at Fort Benning, Ga.—and for that, he was arrested, charged, tried, convicted and sentenced in a federal court in Columbus, Ga.

There will be no appeal. His sentence will be served at a designated federal penal institution, beginning in March.

Beisswenger describes himself as a "post-Holocaust Christian" who believes that "Christian nations can too easily ignore brutality and atrocities done in their name."

The reverend told the court that graduates of the SOA/WHISEC have actively participated in some of the worst human rights abuses on record in Central and South America. Citing such respected sources as Amnesty International—as well as his own serious and prolonged study of the military school and the affected countries—he gave proof that the infamous rape and murder of four missionaries in El Salvador, and the murder of Archbishop Romero there, were committed by men who got their training in counter-terrorism assault tactics at the SOA.

This article originally appeared in "Nashville Eye," *The Tennessean*, September 2, 2004.

You might argue that Beisswenger could have made his point in some fashion other than trespassing outside the place where American military personnel train foreign nationals to conduct "insurgency warfare" against dissidents in their home countries.

But how? In the present atmosphere of hysteria about terrorism, homeland security and other phobias, our government has so insulated and isolated itself from the people and imperiled their basic rights that direct confrontation is the only effective way to make a clear statement of conscience.

And for exercising that right—a right we had assumed was protected by the Constitution and Bill of Rights—Don Beisswenger, an old man in poor health who is certainly no threat to national security, is going to prison. They'll give him a number in place of his name, and he'll sit behind bars for six months.

Brooding about this travesty, I find myself recalling World War II and the number I wore for three years. I was 18 when I got my dog tags with my serial number on it.

As an ordained Baptist preacher, I was exempt from the draft, but I volunteered to serve and spent three years as an infantryman. I learned to shoot guns and to cut and sew on injured soldiers when there weren't enough doctors and nurses.

I didn't know it at the time, but one of the big bombers I saw touch down on a little patch of rock in the South Pacific was the *Enola Gay*, just returning from its history-changing mission over Hiroshima.

Bad as that time was, we're in a worse one now.

This old world is reeling and rocking. We've been lied to and driven into a war of aggression by the leaders of our own government, who justify their actions with slogans:

"Destroy their weapons of mass destruction." Not ours, but theirs. "Destroy the regime of this vicious dictator." Not just any dictator but this particular one. "Rally the coalition of freedom-loving nations." Meaning us and a few more, against the warning of all the others working through the United Nations.

Young men and women with serial numbers just like mine are doing the bloody deeds their commander-in-chief sent them to do, at risk of their lives (more than 500 dead so far) and the lives of the invaded, evil and innocent alike (tens of thousands of them). Such a waste!

How in the name of God can this be justified?

And now Don Beisswenger is going to get his number and enter a prison here in the waning years of his exemplary Christian life.

GREAT GOD!

What are we doing?

Will D. Campbell, a farmer, writer, and Baptist minister of the South, is the author of more than a dozen books. He lives in Mt. Juliet.

Sunday, April 4

A letter to friends and family before leaving for prison

On April 6, I will begin my trek to Manchester, Kentucky, for six months' incarceration, the result of my crossing the line onto Fort Benning to protest the atrocities of SOA/WHINSEC.

The activities of the coming days will be important preparations for my departure. What a gift I have in you, the people who keep providing support and encouragement!

The past months have been productive. I have spoken to groups in Nashville at Belmont University, Vanderbilt University Divinity School, Hillsboro Presbyterian Church, Second Presbyterian Church, the Unitarian/Universalist Church, and the Interdenominational Ministers' Fellowship. What we have done in protesting SOA/WHINSEC has been publicized in articles and radio and television.

My action has provoked interest in SOA/WHINSEC and in our efforts to close the school until an investigation into its complicity in killings, disappearances, and torture has been completed. I encourage you to write your representatives, seeking their sponsorship of House Bill 1258, which seeks a serious investigation of the school. Also, I have received a communiqué about recent actions of SOA/WHINSEC graduates. As far as we can determine, there has been no change in the SOA except its name. The United States has not changed its foreign policy, so any changes to the school are cosmetic. Try to keep yourself informed, using SOA Watch as a resource.

I am grateful for the opportunity to witness on behalf of the victims of SOA/WHINSEC and against the dark side of the United States' military and political history. Pray for our nation that it may recover its commitment to liberty and justice for all.

I do not have an address in prison; so if you wish to write me, send correspondence to my home address. I will not be able to receive phone messages, though I can call collect. Arrangements for communication are difficult. So long, for a time.

[2]
APRIL: ENTERING THE PRISON SYSTEM

We are in a curious position in which a surfeit of prisons filled with a million minority young men is seen not as an embarrassment, but as indispensable to the smooth running of our democracy and integral to its economy. In effect, the attitude that suffused Southern jails and prisons during post-Civil War reconstruction has been replicated nationally.

— JEROME MILLER

Tuesday, April 6, 2004

Today I reported to the U.S. Bureau of Prisons in Manchester, Kentucky. Judy, Cinny, Roger, Philip, and I left Nashville early this morning so we would have time for a picnic in the park and a stop at the Mennonite bakery in Manchester for a snack. Erik Johnson, a former prisoner of conscience, met us with an astonishing array of food and drink for our picnic.

Afterward, we drove to the prison, where I was photographed standing beside the Manchester Federal Prison sign.

We said a prayer and then drove to the maximum security building, where I was to report. Razor wire covered every fence and door. My friends and I held hands and prayed together before I surrendered myself to their *care*, if that is the correct word. If I had not reported, I would have forfeited my bond and would be subject to immediate arrest and a longer sentence.

Outside the federal prison in Manchester

I turned over my papers to a pleasant receptionist and waited for about twenty minutes until a guard escorted me through five steel doors into the maximum security prison. There I was fingerprinted, photographed, and given prison clothes. All the clothes I came with were put into a box to be shipped home. I could keep only my eyeglasses and the two Bibles I brought with me. Written inside the Bibles were the addresses and telephone numbers of persons with whom I wanted to keep in touch.

I brought money to purchase essential personal items: toothpaste, aftershave, fingernail clippers. Electric razors were not permitted, so I purchased shaving cream and razors. Many inmates, I learned, have no one to send them money; so their only funds are the meager wages they earn from prison work. My earnings will be $5.25 per month.

After I was processed, an inmate drove me to the minimum security facility, called "the camp," which would become my home for the next six months. I was taken to an eight-by-ten-foot room with five-foot-high walls made of concrete blocks, and an open space to the ceiling. In my cell is a bunk bed, two lockers, two chairs, a desk, and a bulletin board. I have a lower bunk, a benefit for me as an older person of seventy-three. A two-by-six-foot window in the cell faces a grassy hillside.

The camp is nestled in a valley with high slate and sandstone cliffs on either side. A road at one end leads up to a grassy plateau where there is a softball field, volleyball court, and picnic area. This is a restful place.

Five hundred inmates reside here in four dormitories, with one hundred twenty-five persons in each. The facility is located on a former strip mine. Once the goal was stripping coal from the mountains; now it is stripping life from people as punishment. My roommate is a twenty-six-year-old man from Milwaukee who was sentenced to three months in prison for computer fraud. It is cold tonight. I feel cold inside as well.

Today is the third day of Holy Week, a time encompassing Palm Sunday, Good Friday, and Easter. Before Jesus entered Jerusalem, he wept for the city because the people did not know the way to make peace. Afterward, when he saw profit-making in the Temple, a place of prayer, he became angry and turned over the tables of the money changers. Later, he met with his disciples and prepared for the Passover. The supper must have been marked by confusion, vulnerability, and fear. All the disciples knew was the pounding of their hearts, fear for their own lives, and that this was their last time to be together. Because Jesus was a threat to the Romans as well as to the religious authorities, he would be rejected and crucified. The Jesus story keeps me alive to the mystery of life and death, good and evil, greatness and perversion. It is such a gift!

Thursday, April 8

I received this poem, written by my friend Bill Quigley:

YESTERDAY, MY FRIEND CHOSE PRISON
(Dedicated to the SOA Prisoners of Conscience)

Yesterday my friend walked freely into prison,
chose to violate a simple law to spotlight the evil
of death squads and villages of massacred people we cannot name,
mothers and children and grandparents butchered, buried,
and forgotten by most, but not by my friend.

Yesterday my friend stepped away from loves, family, and friends,
was systematically stripped of everything (everything)
and systematically searched everywhere (everywhere),

was systematically numbered, uniformed, advised, and warned.
Clothes, underwear, shoes, and everything put in a cardboard box,
taped, and mailed away.

Yesterday my friend joined the people we put in concrete and steel boxes:
mothers and children and fathers we cannot name,
in prison for using and selling drugs,
in prison for trying to sneak into this country,
in prison for stealing, scamming, fighting, and killing.
But none were there for the massacres—
no generals, no politicians, no undersecretaries, no ambassadors.

Yesterday my friend put on a brave face,
avoided too much eye contact with the hundreds of strangers,
convicts, prisoners, guards, snitches.
Not yet knowing good from bad,
my friend stayed out of people's business,
hoping to find a small pocket of safety, kindness, and trust in the weeks ahead.

Last night my friend climbed into bed in prison,
an arm's length away from another prisoner,
lying awake on the thin mattress,
wondering who had slept there last,
wondering how loved ones were sleeping,
awake through flashlight bed checks
and never-ending noises echoing off the concrete floors and walls,
some you never, ever want to hear.

Yesterday my friend chose prison over silence,
chose to stand with the disappeared and those who never counted,
chose to spend months inside, hoping to change us outside,
chose to speak truth to power. And power responded with prison.
Though my heart aches for my friend in prison,
no one on this planet is more free.

Friday, April 9

It is Good Friday. The sky is dark as I sit alone at 4:00 a.m. in the TV room,
which has become my quiet place. Arriving early, I can be still and open to
God's Spirit at work in my prison home.

Yesterday I attended an orientation to the prison facility. Wanting to understand the place, I asked questions of each speaker. The other inmates grew angry at the time it took to answer all my questions, especially since I will only be here six months. In the end, we laughed about it. One inmate called me "Pops," as I am older than most.

Saturday, April 10

I am more relaxed. I now have my ID card, and my phone list is completed, though I can't make calls until it is approved.

I turned in my visitors list to my counselor, Mr. Tims, and sent a letter to my son Philip.

I got my pills in order, and the doctor was helpful. I also had my blood sugar checked. It was high again, but under 250, so the doctor said, "No insulin." It will be a task to control my diabetes with diet and exercise. I also got special shoes so that my feet will be cared for.

Easter Sunday, April 11

I entered prison just after Palm Sunday and desired a liturgical framework in which to consider my role here. Today the Southern Baptist minister preached using a text from Ephesians in which Paul speaks of Jesus' suffering, death, and resurrection. However, the sermon focused on "the plan of God," in which Jesus died for our sins according to God's will but with no relationship to human arrogance and power. (The film *The Passion of the Christ* has the same problem.) Jesus' great pain and suffering calls us to worship and praise. I understand Jesus' execution in the context of his challenging the powers of this world, and I celebrate the power of God to bring life out of death. Reducing Jesus' death to personal healing is a gospel that is too small.

All my reflections I hold before you, O God. Help me to see you at work here among the officers, inmates, and staff.

—⟋∿⟍—

Conversational banter consumes much of inmates' time in prison. People also read a lot and sleep. The prison offers a range of activities. The military style of most officers and the rule-oriented nature of the place are in some ways understandable. I have heard about the "hole," a place where inmates are held for major rules violations. I have made several mistakes, but thus far I've only been shouted at. No doubt I'll experience solitary confinement too. The guards demand order.

What most impresses me is the enormous cost of running a prison—facilities, staff, food, clothing, shoes, furniture, recreation. Health care alone, even though it is meager, must be expensive. Everyday meds are distributed; sicknesses and emergencies are addressed; records are kept; doctors, nurses, and technicians are paid.

A Typical Day in Prison

At 6:30 a.m. a voice over the loudspeaker shouts that breakfast is ready. Five hundred men, most in red skullcaps, rush a quarter mile to get in line. The day is cool, so the hats are a bright complement to our beige jackets. We also wear green shirts and green pants with our names and numbers on them in big letters. I bounce along with everyone else to get cold cereal, coffee cake, jam, and coffee.

Near the dining hall is a triangle-shaped grassy area with sidewalks along the outer edges. At 7:00 a.m., after breakfast, we assemble in lines on the sidewalks to be organized for work assignments or to be cursed out for sloppy work the day before. After roll call, we work. My job is to pick up cigarette butts and trash to make the place look neat. I resented the work at first, until I realized I was making my home neater and cleaner. How I conceive of my work makes a difference in how I perform.

Work is interrupted at 10:30 a.m. for lunch. We wait in line for fifteen minutes for a hamburger, lettuce, tomato, french fries, and ice cream, along with a choice of beans, rice, or salad.

After lunch, we go back to work. If my work has been completed by then, I spend the time writing letters or writing in my journal. We return at 2:00 p.m. for our final work report.

In addition to picking up trash, inmates work in the garage, the greenhouse, the carpentry shop, the library, and the law library. From 8:00 a.m. to 3:00 p.m., most prisoners are working. Trash pickup is the first level of work. In several weeks I may be given something else to do.

At 4:00 p.m. the guards take the major prisoner count of the day. We all stand in our cubicles and wait for two guards to check that we are in our cells. Our numbers are added to the Bureau of Prisons' daily national count of the prison population.

We eat supper at 4:30, followed by free time. Classes in Spanish, religion, and preparation for the GED are offered.

Recreation plays a central role here. The softball season has started, so each evening teams gather on the hillside to compete. Four residence halls field the teams. The weight-lifting area is busy all day. Having a strong upper body with many tattoos is a symbol of power for inmates. Bocce is popular here too. The gymnasium consists of a basketball court with bleachers, a game board, a pool table, a treadmill, and a place to play racquetball. Walking is a popular form of exercise. The walk up the hill accelerates my heart rate.

In the evening, we play cards: casino, hearts, spades, cribbage, rummy, and gin. Small groups converse, especially around the microwave. Some inmates are particularly skilled at cooking creative meals. There is one TV room for sports viewing, another for regular programs and news.

—⁓—

A letter to friends and family

My life has settled into a routine here. Much of my energy is still consumed by keeping up with the rules and with scheduled counts, appointments, work, check-ins, and meals.

An article about me in a Nashville newspaper called me an old man who went to jail.[1] I did not like the term *old*, so I asked them to refer to me in the future as *older*. I guess I can't beat the labels.

Inmates mostly segregate by races when eating and talking in groups. I have made a point of relating to everyone, including the several Hispanics who are here. I have had many interesting conversations. Today I talked with a man from northern Indiana, a farmer with six daughters and five grandchildren. He had never been in legal trouble before he let a man grow some "grass" on his

360-acre farm. He was sentenced to four years in prison. It seems he would do well under house arrest, but the laws on drugs are punitive. Ninety percent of the inmates are here for drug-related crimes, usually on charges of conspiracy to sell drugs.

No effort is made to get people to put cigarette butts in ash trays, so we keep picking them up. Since I receive $5.25 a month for the work, it can't be called slave labor. I call it training in irresponsibility.

Visitation is from 8:30 a.m. to 3:00 p.m. on Fridays, Saturdays, and Sundays. I get up to eight points per month to use for visits. Saturday and Sunday visits are two points, and Friday visits are one point. No visits are allowed after the points for the month are used up.

Frances Willard advised, "The world is wide, and I will not waste my life in friction when it could be turned into momentum. I must choose what battles to engage."[2] I will do likewise.

Tuesday, April 13

I got my blood sugar checked—it was down to 134. Great news! It was raining, so the yard cleanup was only half done. Such small tasks for such a large number of folk! Most of the time we did nothing. I went to the library to see about newspapers. There were none. Three are paid for by the library, but they never make it to the library. I talked to another inmate, Shorty, about my teaching a class on the Bible and sexuality. I don't know if the chaplains will approve. Shorty echoes the far right-wing political position on creationism, the NRA, and total militarism. He gave me birthday cards and spiritual cards to use for special events. I worked on getting a cribbage board. Don introduced me to Dick, who beat me in two of three games.

Thursday, April 15

Juson, my roommate for the past ten days, leaves tomorrow. He will be free from this prison; but like all of us, he has his own prisons. The walls we build protect us but also separate us from others. The day will be normal, except that I hope to get my telephone connection completed and to call Judy, Philip, and my friend Bill Barnes. Bill and I, spiritual companions since 1976, continue to meet every week by phone while I am here in prison.

Most inmates are here because they wanted money and took illegal short-cuts to get it. I am here because I resisted my nation's military policies in Latin America. So as a prisoner of conscience I am an odd duck here.

It is difficult to find space to be alone to read, meditate, and pray. The TV room is too noisy, so I am sitting in a corner of the gym. I am grateful for this corner of the world where I can spend some time reading Psalm 70.

Bless the day, O Holy Spirit.

Saturday, April 17

In my time of silence today, God called me to see the inmates as my brothers and to care for them. I read Psalm 71, the prayer of an elderly person. It describes how God leads each person through life. Now that I too am elderly, I pray that God will bless me so that I may be a blessing.

I so enjoy reading, and I finished a novel today. The day was warm, with redbud and cherry trees adding to the beauty of the place. There was no work detail today, so I spent time with my new roommate, Mick, on his fiftieth birthday. He treated the birthday card I gave him with special care by posting it on the bulletin board. He is a talker, but I find him interesting. He has been here before, so he already has friends.

I took a walk with the Catholic chaplain on the upper knoll. We walked around the track talking about my life. It was good to get acquainted.

Sunday, April 18

I am having difficulty being here. My energy is decreasing, my desire to maintain discipline is declining, and I am confused by the daily regimen. I am aware of how much I need to be centered each morning—in God, in the Spirit, and in Christ, the Word made flesh.

Tuesday, April 20

A letter to friends

Thank you to all who have written. Each card and letter brings encouragement and a sense of the community in which I live. This is important to me, especially now at the beginning of my term.

Although I have been here about three weeks, I am still confused about the rules for telephone calls and mail. Head counts take place six to ten times a day, involving a half-mile walk each time. I am getting exercise. My spirit has stayed alive mainly because of your support. Holy presence is here and becomes evident now and again.

My new roommate is from western Kentucky, and I learn from him and others. Most of the inmates come from Kentucky and Tennessee but also from Indiana, South Carolina, Missouri, Ohio, Idaho, Laos, and Mexico. About 90 percent are here on drug-related charges. Because of mandatory sentences, many are in jail on trivial charges. One fellow was given eight years for possession of a small amount of marijuana.

I have become acquainted with many inmates already. I have celebrity status as a prisoner of conscience. Many of the inmates support my dissent, though often from a strong antigovernment bias. They blame the government for all societal problems, including the bombing of Oklahoma City's Murrah Federal Building, which one fellow believes was organized by the government.

> MANY OF THE INMATES SUPPORT MY DISSENT, THOUGH OFTEN FROM A STRONG ANTIGOVERNMENT BIAS.

Religious life here is shaped mainly by southern Christian values and liturgical style. I appreciate the Catholic service since it follows the liturgical year and focuses on the Paschal mysteries.

Continue to pray for oppressed people, especially children; and ask Congress to pass House Bill 1258, a bill to close SOA/WHINSEC until an outside assessment of the graduates' activities is conducted. I rejoice in you, peacemakers, who are called blessed.

Reflections on faith, religion, chaplains, and inmates

There are many religious groups here, and each one is assigned a sponsor. Religious activities are coordinated by three chaplains: a Catholic, the supervising chaplain; a Southern Baptist; and a Missouri Synod Lutheran, who claims to be on the progressive wing of the church. The Lutheran chaplain asked me about A. J. Levine, a Vanderbilt Divinity School professor who teaches New Testament. He heard her lecture on a video course he is taking. We had a good conversation, but when I asked if I might teach a course, he said, "Inmates cannot teach courses."

The following religious groups are approved here: Roman Catholic, Seventh Day Adventist, Jehovah's Witnesses, Buddhist, Hindu, Protestant Christian, Moorish Science, Muslim, Native American, Nation of Islam, Rastafarian, Pentecostal, Spanish Protestant, Shatru, Judaism, House of Yahweh, Hebrew Israelites, Wicca, and Life Connections.

When I receive permission to do so, I plan to participate in a Native American sweat lodge. I have attended several Bible studies and a video presentation on prayer.

Over lunch with two inmates, one formerly a news reporter and the other a fireman, we talked about the Bible. They wondered if our interpretation of the Bible should change to stay current with evolving societal mores. We talked about the need to address the different meanings of words through the centuries. They appreciated the discussion, as did I.

Prior to a softball game a week ago, Stan, one of the inmates, called the team together. He offered this prayer:

Father, who art in heaven: Thank you for this wonderful day. Thank you for the blessings you bestow upon us. Lord, we thank you for looking over our families while we are separated from them. We ask your forgiveness of our sins and wrongdoings throughout this day. Lord, we ask, as we get ready to play this game, that you keep us in character. Put a leash on our tongues so that we will not argue a call. If one of us makes an error, let us do as you said and lift one another up. Lord, we ask for your protection on the field. Keep us from harm or injury, and not only us but the other team as well. Lord, we thank you for this chance to play and to come to you in prayer. We thank and praise you in the name of Jesus. Amen.

This is a small glimpse of religious life here.

Sunday, April 25

The Catholic service today focused on building up one another in faith, rather than on conversion. I have become clearer about how these two perspectives complement each other. Many people are not centered in God or in God's way and need to be invited into the life of faith. Others need encouragement and support, like what was offered at the Catholic service. I need to keep centered and to deepen my understanding of God's ways and God's call to me. The evangelical approach is attractive as a way of bringing some people to start a faith journey. So I think I will participate in both in limited ways.

I called Judy this morning to wish her well on her trip to see an inmate in a women's prison in Memphis whose release we have worked toward for years. Judy has a cooperative and warm spirit. I pray her visit goes well.

Thursday, April 29

My morning was filled with good things: moments of holiness, wonder, passion, and compassion. Why am I blessed with good friends, children, a mission, joy, gratitude, love, even hope—though sometimes hope lags? I weep for the world, so filled with violence, deception, and neglect. *Why are you so powerless, O God? Why do hatred and greed play so much of a role in our culture? I seek to love as you loved. Love abides when all else is gone—hope, faith, knowledge, possessions. Bless this day to your service of love and justice.*

My work assignment was minimal, so I had time to send fifteen letters, most of them copies of a letter I completed earlier. It seems feasible to answer cards and letters in this way. I enjoy being in touch with each person, if only for a brief time.

I am empowered by my connection with the outside world. But the world inside the prison is less empowering for me. I try to be available, supportive, caring, fun, interested, and open while maintaining my identity and making connections with the people here.

Teach me your way, O God. Grant me your light and guidance.

[3]
MAY: SETTLING IN

"I can't live with this constant fear," said Mitra, "with having to worry all the time about the way I dress or walk. Things that come naturally to me are considered sinful, so how am I supposed to act?"

—FROM *READING LOLITA IN TEHRAN*

Saturday, May 1, 2004

I puzzle about who I am here and who I am invited to be with others. Years ago, I wrote this poem:

> Who am I?
> I need to clarify
> who I am each day.
> I cannot be taken for granted.
> Would it not be better
> to get up each morning
> ready to go?
> But I am who I am.

Who am I? I am a seventy-three-year-old man who was married for forty-nine years. I have six children, each of whom I love very much, and eight foster children, only one of whom I still have contact with. I loved my parents, my sisters, and my brother. I worked at Vanderbilt University Divinity School for thirty years.

Who am I here? I am a strong person in some ways. I am able to converse, yet I am reserved. I am a loner who does his own thing, including exercise, tai chi, reading, silent prayer and meditation, and scripture study. I am engaged with several inmates, although on a surface level. I have helped several of them think theologically about their future and their hopes of pursuing a theological education. I participate in the religious life here as an observer. I attend Mass because of its liturgical approach. I enjoy the Catholic chaplain but feel more tension and disagreement with the Baptist and Lutheran chaplains.

An inmate took this snapshot of me and Judy in the visitors' gallery.

I feel loved by many people.

I enjoy writing letters, for they evoke feelings and make me think concretely. I am confused by the rules, and I wonder about my role here. I find Jesus as Christ both a puzzle and a challenge. I find myself asking, *Who is Jesus?* Sometimes I forget to question and simply follow.

I have deep affection for Judy and rely upon her. I enjoy her, love her, care for her; yet I am unsure about marriage. I have enjoyed my freedom and hesitate to give it up.

I continue to be committed to the SOA Watch and its goal of closing the school, and to the Living Room, which offers support to the homeless in Nashville. I am committed but not particularly effective in resisting the war against the poor. I am surprised by the interest in and response to my imprisonment. It seems a modest witness.

Being here is still a puzzle. I try to be a human being among human beings, not an ordained person or a father figure; yet the people here need someone to trust. I resist formal, role-oriented relationships even though I honor role designation in institutions.

I am a human being who seeks to love God with all my heart, mind, and soul; to love my neighbor; to care for myself; and to be a good steward of the earth.

Monday, May 3

At lunch I talked to fellow inmates Mante and Halen about putting together a Bible study on gender and sexuality. They were interested, even though the chaplains objected. I know the first names of about forty inmates and greet them by name to affirm them as people before God.

Cary's mother died yesterday. Many of us signed a card for him. He came over to my cell, and we talked about his feelings of loss. We also talked about his mother's cooking and how she raised seven children. He thinks the photo of my wife, Joyce, looks a bit like his mother. Many inmates dislike Cary because he is an informer. *Bless Cary during this time, O Lord.*

Jerry came down to my cell, and we discussed the Bible. He wants to grow and learn. I am open with him about my views on creation, evolution, and the role of the Bible in the Christian life. I make him think, which is healthy, I believe; but I do not want to disrupt his newfound faith so that he goes back to drugs.

Yesterday I wrote letters during the day, including a long one to Philip about my effort to define my calling here in prison. I went to Catholic mass. In the evening, I attended a Bible study led by Carl, a former gang member who now holds fast to Christ.

Tuesday, May 4

My friend Don Peterson sent me a drawing that seems to be one way of resolving conflict.[1]

There are times when life is restored and the storm of the world becomes calm

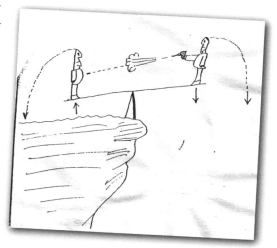

and subject to God's justice, which is shalom. *O Lord, may your kingdom come, your will be done, on earth as in heaven.*

I wrote several letters yesterday, including a lengthy one to Judy, seeking her reflections on our conversation about my role here. I want to know her thoughts about this as well as her reaction to Bonhoeffer's book that includes correspondence with his fiancée.[2] I want our relationship to include intellectual discussion. I enjoyed writing to her. I also wrote a short piece on beauty and the flowers here at the camp. I did not exercise, except to walk up the hill to watch the softball game. It was a good day.

Ryan and I ate supper together, and he told me his story. He learned of a terrorist act being planned by others in his community. He revealed this to the authorities and was charged with involvement in the action. He had a good computer-consulting business, a fine family, a leadership role in the church. Now he feels betrayed by life, by God, and by the government. We read together Psalm 69, which includes this verse: "Do not let those who hope in you be put to shame because of me" (v. 6). I encouraged him to think more broadly about the realities of God. I will try to be present for him.

Wednesday, May 5

Yesterday I had a good early morning. There was little work to do, so I wrote twelve letters and three essays.

> MY LIFE IS
> BLESSED, NOT
> BECAUSE I AM
> GOOD BUT BECAUSE
> GOD HAS LED ME
> IN THE LIFE
> OF FAITH.

I learned today that my work assignment has changed from picking up cigarette butts to serving in the kitchen. I am pleased about the change, because eating is vital to life.

God's abundant grace is a gift for which I give thanks. My life is blessed, not because I am good but because God has led me in the life of faith.

One of the inmates, Jesus, leaves tomorrow. We had an interesting conversation about God, life, and the Bible. Many inmates strongly trust the Bible. I point out the limits of literal interpretation, yet I wonder how vital this is to people who need something solid to hold on to.

I am aware of how much the families of those in prison suffer, more perhaps than the prisoners, who at least have food and shelter.

—∿—

A letter to friends

I have been thinking about you these days, as well as about the people of Latin America. It is raining today, a dreary day at the prison. Yet I feel alive and my spirits are good, mainly because of the community of people with whom I share this journey. You support me in many ways by word, deed, prayers, and letters. You have kept me alive to the beauty of connections with one another, to our strength in times of vulnerability, and to the invitation to work for justice and shalom.

I have been considering my life here. I have time for being, and that is how I start each day. I am also busy doing, as I must work each day. I exercise, even trying a bit of racquetball. I am responding to letters. I spend some time in pastoral care, reading, and socializing. I have tried to keep up with the SOA Watch, and I am glad to know the protest seeking to close the SOA/WHIN-SEC will occur again in Columbus in November. The *New York Times* keeps me informed about the world scene. Another inmate has kindly shared his copy of the newspaper with me, but now I have my own subscription.

I have completed prison orientation and muddled through the confusion of entering this new place. Now God calls me to stillness and waiting to discern what my calling is while I am here.

Many folks have asked how they might help. What I can receive is restricted—no stamps, money, or food. But you can support the SOA Watch and House Bill 1258, which seeks a serious investigation of SOA/WHINSEC.

Friday, May 7

I began my work in the dining room about 11:30 a.m. yesterday, after lunch. I spent most of the time sitting around, trying to figure out what needed to be done. Other people played cards, read, talked. I was bored. I need to bring greeting cards to write and a book to read. I will give this new work time to unfold; a move from being an environmental engineer picking up cigarette butts to being a kitchen engineer will be a challenge—no butts about it!

I did tai chi, some weight lifting, walking, and racquetball. I watched a softball game. My blood sugar was 231 yesterday and 191 this morning. For five days, it was between 70 and 120, and I am unsure what caused the increase. Oh, I ate brownies and some candy last night—now I know.

Sunday, May 9

Yesterday I did not have to work, so I read and slept a lot. I wrote some letters. I felt a bit down. Rainer Rilke says that in new experiences, "our feelings grow mute in shy perplexity, everything in us withdraws, a stillness comes, and the new, which no one knows, stands in the midst of it and is silent."[3]

I have moved into a new phase of my experience here. I no longer struggle so hard to cope with immediate matters. Yet I still have no clarity about my calling in this place.

Friday, May 14

O Lord, I feel troubled. I do not have the joy of your Spirit.

Adell and Ron's racist comments yesterday startled and offended me. My understanding of the social order is not the same as theirs. I seek the unity of life; they seek the domination of life by whites. They feel abused by outside forces. The evil, they think, is government. They do not see government as a reflection of the people—for good or evil. In talking with them, I felt alienated and alienating. Yet we continued to play spades.

God, guide me in relationships with John, Adell, Saxter, Ron, and Matt.

I read an article in *The New Yorker* on the Aryan brotherhood and other gangs in the prison system and how they establish power there. Adell thinks that this view of prison life is made up by eastern Jews and blue bloods. Though I still relate to Adell and enjoy Saxter and Ron, I have taken a step back from these relationships. I anticipated encountering views such as theirs but was surprised by how forceful they are.

I feel adrift. I have a headache from trying to understand myself in this context. I spent time meditating on what I want to do each day. Walking and exercise are important to me, yet I have not established an exercise schedule.

Another inmate, Daniel, told me his story. He grew up smoking marijuana, never thinking of it as a crime. Then to make some money, he sold it and was caught in a conspiracy. He is not in prison for a long time, but his jail time is followed by six months of house arrest. He talked about his contemplative life with God and his interest in Thomas Merton. I enjoyed the time with him.

Bless Dick, my cube mate. He has been pleasant and open to me, even though I am different from the others. Thank you for his grace and insight. Bless his efforts to clarify his time here so that he can leave this place to do your will. Thank you for the great company of folk with whom I share my life. How glorious are your witnesses in all faiths and all backgrounds! Yet we all are broken. We lose direction and become arrogant and rude. Teach me and all your people the ways of love and peace. I pray for the SOA Watch as it witnesses to the truth of atrocities committed by graduates of the school. All this I offer in humble petition, asking that your will be done, on earth as it is in heaven.

Saturday, May 15

Since today is Saturday, I have no work responsibilities. I am free to write letters, to read, and to write in my journal.

Judy came to visit. She had sent me some of her journal entries from 1999, when her husband, Jack, was dying of cancer. Her notes register confusion, contradictory feelings, frustration, sadness, depression. But she cared for him amidst it all. She has a deep and profound loyalty to the claim of relationships.

While Judy was still here, Steve Monhollen came to see me. He is the director of Field Education at Lexington Theological Seminary and a Disciple of Christ. We shared memories of Vanderbilt Divinity School in the 1970s, a time of ferment and experimentation. In those days, before classes began, entering students spent a weekend in the city with only five dollars for expenses. They slept among the homeless; ate where the poor found food; and rode the bus, talking to people. At the conclusion of the weekend, they wrote a brief reflection about the experience.

After the three of us chatted, Steve broke open a small package of crackers and a bottle of grape drink from the vending machine. (Communion bread and drink cannot be brought into the prison.) He asked what came to mind as we partook of the Eucharist in prison. These were my thoughts:

About sixty of the five hundred inmates gather regularly for worship. They speak with gratitude of Jesus, who died for them and who brings healing, power, and love into their lives. They celebrate their new path.

Eucharist is the moment symbolizing and reenacting our reconciliation to God through Jesus. But beyond that, we allow God's love to soak into our heart, mind, body, and spirit. Faith means being grasped by the power of love. I long to help other inmates consider how faith shapes the priorities for their life journeys, their view of women, their lust, and their use of language.

Communion is linked to vulnerability. To be vulnerable is to be aware of possible harm or injury. Prison accents our awareness, especially if we look critically at what is going on around us.

I am reading a biography of Martin Luther King Jr. called Bearing the Cross.[4] *He too felt vulnerable; civil rights activists often experienced cross burnings, house bombings, and even death. Less overt victimization is evident in the culture, which said, "You cannot vote because you did not spell a word properly," or "You did not sign your name in the proper place."*

Jesus was vulnerable. The religious and political forces of his time saw him as a threat, and he was arrested, beaten, mocked, scourged, made to carry his cross, and executed.

The Paschal supper, the Eucharist, demonstrates the relationship of vulnerability and God's word of new life. The resurrection of Jesus is a sign that vulnerability and death do not have the last word. God's will is accomplished.

> TO BE VULNERABLE IS TO BE AWARE OF POSSIBLE HARM OR INJURY. PRISON ACCENTS OUR AWARENESS, ESPECIALLY IF WE LOOK CRITICALLY AT WHAT IS GOING ON AROUND US.

Steve took a cracker, broke it, and said, "This is my body, broken for you." He gave thanks, and we ate the cracker. He took the grape drink and said, "This is my blood, which is poured out for many." We drank and then were silent. Despite all the others in the visitors' gallery, Steve, Judy, and I felt as if only the three of us were there. Steve prayed. It was finished.

Community has come to mean so much to me. Steve's visit was a great joy. Others have visited, written letters, and sent cards. I am caught up in a mighty gathering of compassion, which is inspiring and encouraging.

After Steve left, Judy and I talked a bit longer. We were both tired. Arising at 4:30 a.m. leaves me tired if I don't get an afternoon nap. Judy left to make the four-hour trip home. I returned to my dining room duties: washing tables, sweeping, mopping in preparation for the next meal.

As I reflect on the day, I remember an incident back in 1970. Soon after I arrived at Vanderbilt Divinity School, I helped develop a summer field project in Clairfield, Tennessee, about seventy miles north of Knoxville. The project involved a Danish folk school that focused on building up the sacred life of children, youth, and adults through music, drama, games, activities, and reading. Key leaders in the project were Erling Duus, David Kidd, Gibson Stroupe, and Ed Loring. I met with them one weekend to observe how the summer program was developing and to serve Communion. I celebrated the Lord's Supper, and it carried rich meaning for me. Ed Loring still introduces me by telling of my coming to break bread in the summer of 1970. I could not grasp the significance it held for him. Now I understand.

BECAUSE THERE IS A GEOGRAPHY TO THE LIFE OF FAITH, WHERE WE STAND AFFECTS WHAT WE SEE.

Because there is a geography to the life of faith, where we stand affects what we see. The broken bread and the common cup give testimony to the power of God. The Spirit, a holy presence, comes to us. The spirit of Jesus, who died and lives, comes again into the community. In these truths our hope abides.

Sunday, May 16

I attended the Protestant worship service to hear the Lutheran chaplain speak. In the sermon, he spoke of Jesus' ministry and of the wonderful diversity of God's creation. Each of us, created in the image of God, is given unique gifts.

Carl, an inmate, stood during the prayer time to speak. He said his granddaughter was no longer a lesbian but had chosen heterosexuality. He was glad and praised God.

I was aware that his praise was genuine, yet I felt it would make gay or lesbian people feel unwelcome at the service. The beauty of diversity honored by the chaplain in the sermon was jettisoned; sexual diversity was rejected. Furthermore, the chaplain spoke to Carl and confirmed the importance of his testimony. He talked about Exodus International, which aims to help people change from homosexuality to heterosexuality. The chaplain's statements further alienated gay men—they were not welcome unless they changed. I thought of speaking up but did not. Instead I wrote a memo to the chaplains— my small act of resistance! I indicated I could no longer participate in the service, because exclusiveness is not of God.

I pray, O God, for your wisdom. Help me to avoid pride or easy judgment. O God, bless Carl, his granddaughter, and the chaplains. May light come from my witness.

Thursday, May 20

Yesterday Dick and I reported to Mr. Hull, the unit manager. He told us that our room was a mess. "There is dust on the windows and clutter on your desk, all over the bed, and on top of lockers. You do not deserve a room." Then he told us to pack up and move into the hall. That was it—no warning, though he checked our cubicle each week.

We moved to a bunk bed in an area between the microwave and the telephone. I thought it would be difficult to sleep, but I slept well last night.

Mr. Hull did not give us a chance to explain the condition of our room. I was more at fault than Dick. I had not followed the rule about having nothing on the bed and nothing on the desk except a Bible. Clutter is normal for us, and we do not dust well. I left things in piles, intending to organize them later. I did not understand the seriousness of the rules.

I was angry about our eviction and read Psalm 140 to the inmates in the dorm as a protest: "Deliver me, O LORD, from evildoers . . . ." Dick seemed to relish the discipline, but I felt vulnerable. For the first time since I checked in, I felt I could be hurt or injured.

So far we are making it, but living in the hall is difficult. All my clothes are hanging from the bed. My books and writing materials are in boxes under the bed. It is difficult to focus on reading or writing.

I feel violated by Mr. Hull's examination of our cubicle. He must have looked through my papers and read them. He could have read this journal. I feel exposed. I wonder what other forms of surveillance operate here. I want to ask the Chief, an inmate, about the time Mr. Hull spent in my cubicle.

Mr. Hull has a job to do and he is doing it. The rules are central. I wonder if we are being watched in the visitors' gallery.

—⟋⟍—

Our first memo to Mr. Hull, unit manager

> You have disciplined us for the dirt and clutter in our cubicle, OB 123, by requiring us to sleep in the hall.
>
> We acknowledge and accept that our room was disorderly and that the windowsill was dusty. The importance of order and cleanliness is now clear to us, and we intend to be diligent in keeping the desk and beds clear, the sill dusted, and the floors clean. We have cleaned the windowsill and mopped the floor. We will continue to do this regularly in the future.
>
> We ask that we be reinstated to our room. We would be grateful if we were permitted to move back in to sleep and to store our belongings.
>
> Again, we regret causing difficulties for you and the prison.

Mr. Hull responded that we had not been disciplined, but our living arrangement had simply changed. Furthermore, he said he would consider moving us to another cubicle "when it is convenient for me."

We lived in the hall for five weeks.

[4]
JUNE: SURVIVING

*I feel like I'm walking down a new path. . . . It is a sense of helpless-
ness—that I who always wanted to be the champion of the poor am just
as helpless—that I, too, must hold out my begging bowl; that I must
learn—am learning—the ultimate powerlessness of Christ. It is a
cleansing experience. So many things seem less important, or not at all,
especially the ambitions.*

—PENNY LERNOUX

Thursday, June 3, 2004

This morning, I began to read *The Spiral Staircase*, by Karen Armstrong.[1] The
book tells of her move from a convent into the secular world and her difficulties adjusting, which led to mental illness and physical disability.

Armstrong's book compares life in the convent with life in the world. In
the convent, everything has sacred significance; in the world, nothing seems to
matter. Though freedom leads Armstrong to defy her past, she must create a
new reality for herself.

The new reality—"the unrestrained, babbling roar of four hundred students"—assaulted Armstrong; yet she kissed the floor out of joy for her new
freedom—or perhaps from habit.[2] In the convent, she failed to find God, but
it proved a fixed point of orientation, a home. Now nothing was a given, only
options that led to stunned bewilderment. In the convent, she felt isolated and

alone; her capacity for affection atrophied, her heart hardened. She became a person who could not love.

Isolation is central to the initiation process in the convent. Is the purpose of isolation to make a person independent or pliable? Armstrong says that in the convent she was unable to accept love. "I had wanted to be transformed and enriched; instead I was diminished. Instead of becoming strong, I was simply hard."[3]

And what about prison? Does it also create people who cannot love?

Sunday, June 6

Excerpt from an unsent letter to friends and supporters

I am reading about prison life and the prison system. Protesting the government's military policies is not in keeping with the patriotism of our time. My walk of six steps onto Fort Benning led to a six-month sentence, a fine, and the loss of Social Security benefits—a stringent penalty for dissent. Excessive sentences and penalties, even for nonviolent crimes, are now the rule. Conspiracy—and implicating other people to get a lighter sentence—is the key to many convictions and the grounds for a dangerous social system. Conspiracy laws have led to a radical increase in our prison population since the "tough on crime" years began in the 1980s. At the same time, privatization of prisons began, and they became profitable businesses. I have learned that most of the food items stored in the warehouse here have expired "sell by" dates. The criminal justice system is now a rich source of cheap labor, a way to control dissent, and a means of funneling private funds to increase profits.

Yesterday I was reading at a picnic table on the inmates' playing field. Three men came over to sit in the sun, and I overheard their conversation. One said to the other, "Why don't you have a tattoo on your arm like this?" He pointed to a barbed wire design tattooed around his arm.

The other answered, "I'm not into that."

The third man protested as if he were recruiting for an organization. "You need to get a tattoo!" (Two or three inmates do tattoos at the prison.) He had a spider web tattooed on his whole arm with his elbow at the center of the web; I've heard that the tattoo is a symbol of fascism. "My next tattoo," he said, "will be a skull with a Confederate flag coming out of it and a Klan cap on top."

I am not unduly afraid, yet I am aware of the reality of prison, both in its operation and its population. Nevertheless, I still rejoice at the power of life, its wonders, its diversity.

I remain concerned about the SOA/WHINSEC. The same atrocities present in Iraqi prisons are commonplace in Latin America. As a nation, we know how to terrorize. We have terrorized Native Americans, African Americans, Latinos, and dissenters. I remain angry; but I am also filled with wonder at the beauty of people, even here in an old strip mine turned into a prison.

Friday, June 11

A letter to friends

Newspapers come infrequently here. The library receives neither newspapers nor magazines. Word travels slowly. I finally heard that former President Ronald Reagan has died and that the funeral is today.

Reagan was, to many, a sincere man; but I consider him sincerely wrong.

A friend pointed out a quotation from Dietrich Bonhoeffer, written on New Year's Day 1943:

> Folly is a more dangerous enemy to the good than evil. One can protest against evil; it can be unmasked and, if need be, prevented by force. Evil always carries the seeds of its own destruction, as it makes people, at the least, uncomfortable. Against folly we have no defence. Neither protests nor force can touch it; reasoning is no use; facts that contradict personal prejudices can simply be disbelieved—indeed, the fool can counter by criticizing them, and if they are undeniable, they can just be pushed aside as trivial exceptions. So the fool, as distinct from the scoundrel, is completely self-satisfied; in fact, he can easily become dangerous, as it does not take much to make him aggressive. A fool must therefore be treated more cautiously than a scoundrel; we shall never again try to convince a fool by reason, for it is both useless and dangerous.[4]

This quotation seems apt for Reagan, but more so for George W. Bush. Reagan seemed to have no grasp of the broader picture of life on this planet; neither does Bush. So they have engaged in what Bonhoeffer calls folly. Both are described as decisive and persistent, and that seems sufficient for some people. But they have engaged in folly and are fools—dangerous fools.

I receive courage from knowing that God is the only one before whom I bow and that God's purposes are sure and not to be confused with my apprehension of them.

God seems absent from prisons, whether in Iraq or here in Manchester, yet sometimes I see signs of grace, and I am grateful for this. Though many bow down to and find meaning in the abomination of war, scripture says, "You who fear the LORD, trust in the LORD! He is their help and their shield" (Ps. 115:11).

I found the following quotation from Bonhoeffer helpful when my wife, Joyce, died.

> First: nothing can make up for the absence of someone whom we love, and it would be wrong to try to find a substitute; we must simply hold out and see it through. That sounds very hard at first, but at the same time it is a great consolation, for the gap, as long as it remains unfilled, preserves the bonds between us. It is nonsense to say that God fills the gap; he doesn't fill it, but on the contrary, he keeps it empty and so helps us to keep alive our former communion with each other, even at the cost of pain.
>
> Secondly: the dearer and richer our memories, the more difficult the separation. But gratitude changes the pangs of memory into a tranquil joy. The beauties of the past are borne, not as a thorn in the flesh, but as a precious gift in themselves. We must take care not to wallow in our memories or hand ourselves over to them, . . . but . . . keep [them] simply as a hidden treasure that is ours for certain. In this way the past gives us lasting joy and strength.[5]

Saturday, June 12

I received a letter from a teenage girl that lifted my spirits:

Dear Reverend Don Beisswenger,

My name is Javiera Vergara. I am seventeen years old and attend Immaculate Heart of Mary High School in Berwyn, Illinois. Last November, I too attended the SOA/WHINSEC protest. That was a weekend that changed my life forever.

It's funny how life seems so simple, but it really isn't. Humans are complex beings that can do things so wonderful and beautiful and yet be capable of mass destruction. Going to the protest made me angry, and it also made me feel useless. Things that I thought could be figured out simply are too complex even to think about sometimes. People tend to be so freaking greedy and totally oblivious to those around them; it hurts me deep inside—more, I think, than it hurts other kids my age. But what can we do unless we have money? I pray—but I don't think it will do any good. I mean, God did give everyone free will. It's too bad so few people have learned to love; they are too wrapped up in money to see clearly.

But I still pray and ask God to help me not to be afraid of the future of our world. I pray that God will give others good judgment and will let them see how wonderful it is to love others. It's too bad many people won't have the chance.

Well, I have to go, but I wanted to finish by saying that I think it's great that you crossed the line. I hope you are doing fine, and may God give you all of God's blessings. You are a wonderful person. Let's keep praying. I know I need prayers if I'm going to survive here on earth. And of course, let's pray that the school closes. Thanks for reading, and God bless.

Love,

Javiera Vergara

Sunday, June 13

Memo to the chaplains

I have just returned from the Protestant worship service and thought I would write to you about my experience.

1. I feel left out. I do not find the liturgy conducive to the worship of God because it is oriented toward evangelism, and I have been a believer for over sixty-five years. I know I am unusual in some ways, but I imagine there are others who seek to grow in the Christian life and seek to understand its meaning for their personal life, their interpersonal life, and the public world. What does the faith say about issues related to the earth, war, peace, violence, abuse of power, and prisons?

2. To focus only on coming to faith by acknowledging our self-centeredness and holding fast to God, whom Christians see most clearly in Jesus Christ, is to ignore faith that seeks understanding and tangibility in life. I find little

help in the worship service. Such matters may be mentioned in prayer, but are not spelled out much in sermons. Public issues are addressed only to make a point. For instance, Jesus tells us to be peacemakers and to love our enemies. I take the scripture to mean that we do not kill our enemies. Any talk of corporate or national self-righteousness is absent. The wondrous nature of the life of faith is reduced to personal theology and morality.

3. I like the scriptures to be read according to a regular pattern, not according to the minister's choice. On Good Friday, the story of the Crucifixion was not read. Could the Lutheran pastor lead a Protestant service based on the Lutheran liturgy as an alternative to the Southern Baptist service? I also like to receive the Lord's Supper regularly.

4. The teaching ministry is also oriented to conservative theology. The series on creation and evolution was slanted; the series on prayer was shaped by a particular view of salvation. The Bible studies tend toward fundamentalism, and this viewpoint is not mine. Though I have gone to several studies, I have found that my questions upset others in the class.

I cannot participate in the worship or teaching here, though I have given it a try. As you know, I also have problems with services that have not welcomed gay Christian men.

I write this letter as one person's assessment.

Friday, June 25

A letter to family and friends

I've put on my bulletin board a picture of Dorothy Kazel, one of four women missionaries who were raped and killed in El Salvador on December 2, 1980. The picture reminds me that I am here to witness against atrocities committed in our [country's] name. We know that atrocities are common in military situations where secrecy protects violence and torture.

The goal of SOA Watch remains the same: to shut down SOA/WHIN-SEC until a serious effort is made to discover activities by graduates of the school. The "one bad apple" interpretation of events—also used in Iraq—seeks to cover up reality. A recent study shows that the more courses people have taken at the school, the more human rights violations they have committed.

For a long time, our nation has been involved in training people in terrorist tactics. Now it is often hidden by the secrecy of the CIA or the armed services. Fortunately, we still find out what goes on, but secret terrorism remains pervasive.

I just received word that the Foreign Appropriations Bill is moving to the House

Sister Dorothy Kazel

soon. It is scheduled to be advanced prior to the recess on July 23. We must have at least 150 cosponsors for the amendment requiring investigations into SOA/WHINSEC and its graduates. We do not want to risk losing by a large vote, so please contact your representatives. We should have responded to information about prison abuse in Iraq. In the same way, the military operates without accountability in Latin America.

My roommate and I have been living in the hall about a month now. We have adapted and find our lives reasonably normal even though we live, dress, and sleep in what is called the "bus stop."

May you be blessed in the struggle for justice. Supreme Court Justice Anthony Kennedy spoke last fall calling for repeal of mandatory minimum sentences, in which case most of the people here would be free. We need to support changes in the justice system.

Don

P.S. from Judy

Since Don wrote this letter, he has been allowed to move back into a room; and at least for the moment, he has it all to himself. I am truly amazed at the number of inmates who talk to him, comment on how he helps them, and befriend him. Although there have been some difficult incidents, Don has handled these problems with equanimity. We are now over the hump in his time of imprisonment. Blessings to all who send letters, cards, and prayers of encouragement to Don.

Saturday, June 26

I have moved beyond "shy perplexity" and have begun to feel right being here. I have listened to my feelings and inclinations as well as to my environment to find out what I am called to do and be. The Spirit provokes me and keeps me alive, deepening the stirrings of truth, love, and hope in my life.

I have been encouraged to spend the next month in a kind of monastic retreat, but that will be difficult both because of who I am here and the nature and the demands of the setting in which I live. However, in various ways, my activities express my calling to love God, to love my neighbor, to love myself, and to work toward a community in which all people love one another.

No particular place is needed to pursue my calling; each place becomes important as I am attentive to it. As I review my daily schedule, I realize that nothing is unusual about it. Nevertheless, in my ordinary life, there is mystery, wonder, and complexity.

Sunday, June 27

I just returned from the Catholic liturgy. Before the service, I told them that fifty years ago today, Joyce and I were married. Recently I wrote this letter to my children.

> Dear Rebecca, Suzanne, Philip, Tom, Drew, Siram, and your families,
> Joyce and I were married in Osage, Iowa, on June 27, 1954. This year would have been our fiftieth anniversary. While Joyce and I did not reach fifty years together, I want to celebrate the moment, remembering with great appreciation the life we had together.
> We had a remarkable life. We had six fine children, eight grandchildren, and eight foster children. You, our children, were the center of our life and the focus of our energy and commitment. You were a joy to both of us. Penuel Ridge Contemplative Retreat Center was a dream we shared, but Joyce persisted in seeing it through. Our purpose for the retreat center was

My family at Thanksgiving, November 2002. Joyce and I are in the second row.

to offer opportunities for people to encounter the love of God, neighbor, and self, and experience the integrity of all creation.

Joyce has a permanent place in my heart. I continue to deal with the loss of her friendship and companionship. She loved me, and I was grateful. I loved her, and she was grateful. It takes a long time to make such good wine. We were both human, which made our lives interesting. We changed as we grew. Our commitment to each other was strong. Joyce will always be a part of our family, and she will bless us with her spirit of goodness and compassion.

I send my love and joy at our sacred memory.

Dad

Monday, June 28

On Friday, I had three visitors from Nashville: Reverend Will Campbell, a noted author who is about eighty years old and uses a cane for balance; John Egerton, also a noted writer; and Matt Leber, director of a nonprofit agency. I was excited about the visit.

An inmate took this picture of me with authors John Egerton and the Reverend Will Campbell.

When I arrived at the visitors' area to meet them, an officer confronted me. He was angry and of a mind to cancel my visit because Matt was wearing sandals and socks, and sandals are not permitted. He shouted at me, saying that it was my responsibility to tell my visitors what to wear. Then he threatened, "I intend to do everything in my power to have your visitor privileges revoked."

Will and John said that Matt had been told to wait in the parking lot. Will, visibly shaken by his encounter with the officer, cried for a time. John was angry because of the officer's disrespect. Our visit continued for a while, and finally Matt arrived wearing new sneakers that he had purchased in town.

As we concluded our time together, Will said that he hoped he would not cry on the next visit. It was a sad end to our time together.

I filed a complaint asking that the officer be punished for his actions, and that he be dismissed as an officer in charge of visitation. The associate warden responded to my complaint with an apology and an admission that "visitors are authorized to wear sandals in the visiting area."

Wednesday, June 30

A letter to my visitors

Dear Will, John, and Matt,

Thank you for coming to visit me. Contact with friends like you keeps my spirit alive and well. As you can imagine, I do have down days and need contact with friends so that I don't feel alone. I regret the events of Friday. They are normal for prison life. Authority and discipline are appropriate in social institutions, but power often leads to domination and abuse.

The officer you encountered talks like a drill sergeant and enforces all the rules meticulously. He has been known to burst into the dorm, throwing clothes on the floor and dumping out boxes. He will put inmates in solitary for minor rules infractions. There are a million rules that can be called upon to demean or punish inmates.

Yet I am in good spirits. I enjoyed our time together. We laughed and told stories. We found some joy despite the difficult beginning of our visit. You are special people in my life.

Grace and shalom,

Don

—⚞—

A colleague sent me this poem by Vassar Miller. Posted on my bulletin board, it came to mean much to me.

WITHOUT CEREMONY
Except ourselves, we have no other prayer;
Our needs are sores upon our nakedness.
We do not have to name them; we are here.
And You who can make eyes can see no less.
We fall, not on our knees, but on our hearts,
A posture humbler far and more downcast;
While Father Pain instructs us in the arts
Of praying, hunger is the worthiest fast.
We find ourselves where tongues cannot wage war
On silence (farther, mystics never flew)
But on the common wings of what we are,
Borne on the wings of what we bear, toward You,
Oh Word, in whom our wordiness dissolves,
When we have not a prayer except ourselves.[6]

(5)
JULY: BEING CONFINED

O Great Spirit,
Whose voice I hear in the winds,
And whose breath gives life to all the world,
Hear me! I need your strength and wisdom.

FROM A NATIVE AMERICAN PRAYER

Saturday, July 3, 2004

I am grateful for the depth of community within which I abide. I have been overwhelmed by letters I've received from all over the country and from many people I do not know. The Catholic Worker community keeps me aware of other prisoners of conscience. I have heard from Liz McAlister at Jonah House and from Bill Coffin.

With Judy's help, I have been able to make my Medicare payments, give a gift to Penuel Ridge in honor of Joyce and our fifty years together, and secure commissary funds for snacks and stamps.

I am writing to those gathering for the Peace Breakfast at the Presbyterian General Assembly in Charlotte, North Carolina. I want to greet them and express my appreciation for the honor of the 2004 Peaceseekers Award, given to those who are or have been prisoners of conscience. I will try to find someone to accept the award for me. I am grateful to be part of the body of Christ, the Presbyterian community, and especially the Presbyterian Peace Fellowship. They have been a mighty presence for me through my arrest, arraignment, trial, and imprisonment. Jesus said that the peacemakers are blessed. We are blessed, especially when we have one another and a common trust in the love and power of the Holy One.

Wednesday, July 7

I met with Mr. Jobe, my caseworker, and Mr. Hull, the unit manager. Mr. Jobe asked about my plans after I leave in October. I told him that I would continue to protest the war against the poor in Nashville and in Latin America. He asked why people are homeless; and I replied that a lack of affordable housing, living wages, and jobs keeps people poor.

Mr. Jobe mentioned my time of living in the hall. I said that I had learned the rules on neatness after five weeks without a desk, light, locker, or coatrack. My sister Mitzi laughed when she heard I was put in the hall—at seventy-three years of age!

I've settled on using the laundry room for reading and writing. I unpack my box at 4:15 a.m. At 6:30 a.m. I pack up and leave. I always make myself a cup of tea.

I feel uneasy about using the room. Jay came in and worked at his laundry assignment, but he was quiet and accepted my presence. Stuart even pulled out a large cardboard box for me to use as a desk and another box for me to sit on.

I am grateful for the other inmates' support when we lived in the hall. They were sometimes noisy, but they quieted down when we asked. I am amazed that we adjusted as well as we did. My roommate and I retired at 9:00 p.m. after the last count. We had no light to read by, so sleep was the best option.

My resentment toward Mr. Hull has dissipated (we are called to pray for enemies), but I do not appreciate him. I know that he used punishment for minor violations to assert his power.

I am more afraid of the guards' power. I wonder what will happen next. On my bulletin board is Romans 8:38-39: "I am convinced that neither death, nor life, nor angels, nor rulers, nor things present, nor things to come, nor powers, nor height, nor depth, nor anything else in all creation, will be able to separate us from the love of God in Christ Jesus our Lord."

I pray Psalm 23:4: "Even though I walk through the darkest valley, I fear no evil; for you are with me."

Friday, July 9

Manny, in his late twenties, keeps up a lively, often brutal, stream of conversation and shouting from his top bunk. His banter is violent and demeaning. I keep my distance, but on occasion he directs a barb at me.

On Friday morning, I did not get any letters at mail call. Since I always receive some mail, not getting any made me uneasy. So I went around the dorm asking about the mail. Had it gotten lost or misplaced?

When I came to Manny's cubicle, he said, "Beisswenger, why in hell are you worried about not getting mail? You get mail every day. On the one day you don't, you get all out of joint. Just cool it!"

I reacted to his belittling of my concerns by saying, "Manny, why don't you just shut up! You don't know what you're talking about."

Manny countered, repeating what he had said before. "Why are you so concerned? You get mail all the time."

We continued to shout at each other. Other inmates gathered in the aisle and listened, wide-eyed, to our argument. Seeing us argue gave them joy.

After I thought about it, I was glad I took on Manny and stood my ground. From that point on, Manny and I had a better relationship.

Monday, July 12

The body, exercise, and the weight room

Each morning after a light breakfast, I exercise. I begin with the weight machines and free weights, strengthening my knees, shoulders, and arms. Lifting weights is invigorating, a good way for me to start the day. Afterward, I do several stretching exercises, push-ups, and then tai chi.

I realize why Nelson Mandela worked out during his twenty-nine years in prison. He is a model for me in keeping my body strong and my mind and spirit focused on freedom for brothers and sisters.

When I arrive at the weight room, six people are already there. One man shouts a lot while exercising. Another advises me on how to improve my routine, which is modest in comparison to his. The inmates work out to build their upper-body strength and to win approval when they get out of prison. I work out as a way to pass the time and to keep my body strong.

Other inmates exercise by walking and running. Each night there is a parade of people walking or running around the compound, up the hill to the recreation area, and around it several times. Some people run ten miles a day.

Some prisoners are seriously overweight when they arrive. One forty-year-old man, here on marijuana charges, weighed about 300 pounds when he came in, and already has lost nearly 100 pounds.

Team sports—especially basketball and softball—also provide exercise. Between six and eight softball teams play each week. I tried softball and played right field. It has been a long time since my youth, when I played regularly each summer. I was sad to discover that I could not play well enough to enjoy or add to the game. In one game I caught a fly ball but failed to close the glove, so I dropped it. I picked up the ball to throw it to the second-base man, but I couldn't throw overhand because of a shoulder injury. My effort went about fifteen feet. My batting wasn't much better. I made three hits, each six feet, but I circled the bases and scored a run. After that, I settled for watching, which I enjoyed.

I also watched bocce and basketball games. The basketball league consists of eight or nine teams that play each week. There are many fine players who can pass and shoot like pros.

Here bocce is played on a ten-by-sixty-foot court, with balls the size of croquet balls and another ball called the pea, which is twice the size of a golf ball. The pea is thrown down the court; then players throw the larger balls and earn points by coming close to the pea. When the pea and another ball touch, it is called a bocce and is awarded three points. Eleven points wins the game. I played a few times and enjoyed it.

Most inmates say they play games to help pass the time and avoid boredom. But for many, exercise and sports give life meaning by awarding status to the better players. Exercise is also a way of dealing with stress, containing anger, and controlling violence. During a softball game, one player attacked the third-base man with a bat. Both were sent to the solitary housing unit.

God has given each of us a body integrally related to who we are. Exercise is not only for the body but also for the spirit—for the whole person. People are created, body and spirit, in God's image. We are responsible for keeping ourselves healthy. At a deeper level, we do not finally focus on ourselves but on God's love toward us, which is gracious, truthful, and potent.

Wednesday, July 14

Now that survival has become less of a concern, I have begun to think more about confinement. The character of my confinement has changed. It is not as much something out there, over against me, as it is a state of being.

In the novel *Boy's Life* by Robert McCammon, the eleven-year-old protagonist says,

> I realized all prisons were not buildings of gray rock bordered by guard towers and barbed wire. Some prisons were houses whose closed blinds let no sunlight enter. Some prisons were cages of fragile bones, and some prisons had bars of red polka dots. In fact, you could never tell what might be a prison until you'd had a glimpse of what was seized and bound inside.[1]

Although confinement is still a physical reality, my spirit moves beyond this place. My work in the dining room is boring, and my routines seem empty except for the two hours of prayer and meditation in the early morning. That is a grace-filled time.

Relating to Judy has become more central to my life. She has been such a dear. Silence before such mysteries seems correct, so I shall be silent.

Tuesday, July 20

A letter to my support group

I encourage you to write Congressman Jim Cooper, asking him to become a cosponsor of House Bill 1258. The following form letter may be used to address Congressman Cooper and others in Congress.

> Dear Mr. Cooper:
> I ask that you become a cosponsor of House Bill 1258. The Abu Ghraib prison atrocities show us what can happen when we ignore signs of abuse by military personnel. The presence of private contractors in Iraq and other nations makes our oversight more critical. Serious investigation into the activities of graduates of SOA/WHINSEC is also essential to the establishment of justice for all. We suffer now because we have ignored the results of past investigations.
> Sincerely,

In a recent letter to a constituent, Congressman Cooper expressed support for SOA/WHINSEC. This is disappointing, indeed tragic, in light of the Iraqi prison atrocities. He said that SOA/WHINSEC performs an important function by bringing military personnel to the United States for teaching and by promoting greater respect for human rights in Latin America. Further, he said the Department of Defense has changed the curriculum and focus of the institution. He claimed all this without data from outside investigation.

In the epilogue to Nat Hentoff's book *The War on the Bill of Rights* is this quotation from a letter Supreme Court Justice William O. Douglas once wrote to a group of young lawyers:

> As nightfall does not come all at once, neither does oppression. In both instances, there is a twilight when everything remains seemingly unchanged. And it is in such twilight that we all must be most aware of change in the air—however slight—lest we become unwitting victims of the darkness.[2]

I fear the twilight is upon us, and even more terrible darkness could come. We need to speak while we have the opportunity to do so.

Thursday, July 22

Here are some items on my to-do list:

- write to a friend about a *New York Times* article
- send a reflection to the Open Door
- secure money to buy stamps and postcards
- contact people who want visitor forms approved
- thank Judy for sending letters to two people in prison
- reflect on Romans 5:1 ("Therefore, since we are justified by faith, we have peace with God through our Lord Jesus Christ.") and on how the Spirit teaches us to pray
- write a letter to SOA/WHINSEC compatriots

—🙵—

In his book *God Has a Dream*, Bishop Desmond Tutu reflects on human freedom, a subject of great interest for me in prison. He suggests that God has given us space to be human beings, with the autonomy to say yes or no to God.

Such freedom is necessary, he suggests, for a relationship with God to be grounded in love rather than in coercion or legalism. Thus, to be human is to be free. Moral responsibility makes no sense without freedom, Tutu believes. God took great risk in creating us to be free, but this freedom is the ground for life. Freedom of movement, association, and expression are all essential. These cannot be eradicated, he argues. The yearning for freedom is a yearning to be human. Tutu writes, "This is what tyrants and unjust rulers have to contend with. They cannot in the end stop their victims from being human."[3]

The struggle for freedom becomes central within a prison. Here persons are confined in small spaces, are often disrespected, and seek to be free of such constraints, even if it means challenging the rules. I agree with Tutu that prisons will ultimately fail because they deny something that cannot be denied.

Saturday, July 31

A friend sent me a poem by R. S. Thomas. "The Presence" tells of the power that is with us "before [we] perceive it, sunlight quivering on a bare wall."[4]

[6]
AUGUST: REFLECTING

To be grateful for the good things that happen in our lives is easy, but to be grateful for all of our lives—the good as well as the bad, the moments of joy as well as the moments of sorrow, the successes as well as the failures, the rewards as well as the rejections—that requires hard spiritual work.

—HENRI NOUWEN

Tuesday, August 3, 2004

A reflection on pastoral care in prison

Inmates suffer many losses. Perhaps most difficult is the loss of daily contact with family. And when a spouse and an inmate divorce, contact with the children becomes difficult.

They also lose jobs and wonder how their financial needs will be met upon their release. How will they replace houses, cars, clothes, and savings?

Finally, they experience a loss of community that gives life meaning. Inmates are alone and often forgotten. Sixty percent of the people here never receive a letter. Even when relationships with family and friends are strong to begin with, they are hard to maintain in prison.

These losses breed anger, confusion, aggression. Without hope, inmates sink into an emotional numbness, a deep and pervasive despair. After a time, the numbness lifts and inmates focus on activities such as body-building and sports to help pass the time.

Whenever loss occurs, grief results; and it needs attention. What sort of pastoral care will help inmates deal with loss? Here are some ideas to consider:

- A pamphlet of daily readings would help inmates deal with grief.
- A support group might be formed so that people dealing with loss can talk about their experience.
- Escape from feelings may be necessary for a time. However, learning from loss is perhaps more constructive. What has loss done for us? How can we describe our feelings? Sometimes blame or anger at a spouse or a snitch takes over, but these feelings are ways of avoiding loss and devastating grief. Safe opportunities to struggle with and to learn from loss and grief should be offered.
- Loss sometimes leads to acquisitiveness, a desire to buy lots of stuff. Most of the people here are in prison because they took shortcuts to getting money. Helping inmates view money responsibly is important. So is helping them find ways to deal with loss in constructive ways.

Thursday, August 5

On most mornings I have such a sense of gratitude. My urinary tract works. My bowels work. The razor works. All these are blessings for which I regularly give thanks. My readings are helpful in centering my thoughts and connecting me to the larger human story. What a gift! In the evening, I write letters and cards to various folks.

A reflection on my morning readings: We preach the good news of Jesus not because people need to know Jesus in order to enter the kingdom of God, but because we want to express the love and hope of Jesus Christ.

Friday, August 6

Judy is coming to visit today, as are Bill and Margaret Howell.

The physician indicated that I am in good health. Blood pressure good; diabetes okay, though it could be better; weight okay. I will have the mole on my face checked.

Saturday, August 7

Judy is coming again today, along with Philip and Bacilia. I look forward to the day.

I rejoice in having fresh peaches to eat these past weeks.

I asked some of my inmate friends to have their pictures taken with me. I had to ask them three times; folks forget, and I have to round them up again.

Sunday, August 8

My conversation with Judy was a joy. We talked about the garden at the condo; my loss of Social Security benefits; upcoming birthdays and visits; Will Campbell's book about Robert Clark's journey to the Mississippi legislature[1]; the Living Room, a weekly gathering of homeless people; Judy's grandchildren who are visiting. I am comfortable with her; I don't have to prove myself any longer.

Pope Paul VI said, "The Church looks at the world with profound understanding, with sincere admiration, and with sincere intention, not of dominating it, but of serving it, not despising it, but appreciating it, not condemning it but strengthening it and saving it."[2] As a Christian, I seek to look at other people and to live in these ways. In discovering my own inwardness, I am in communion with all other human beings, as well as with nature, beauty, and goodness. I am part of the human story and the earth's story.

Monday, August 9

I asked Red why he was hostile to me when I complained about smoking in the bathroom. He said, to begin with, that he had stopped smoking. Then he said that he felt I had disregarded the care he took to spray air freshener after he smoked. We reconciled a bit, and I feel a growing relationship with him.

Tuesday, August 10

In the morning, I wrote a page on pastoral care in the prison and sent it to Janet Wolf. I also wrote to Rep. Jim Cooper expressing my concerns about SOA/WHINSEC.

Saxter and I had a discussion on how parental behavior affects children. He feels that adults excuse themselves by blaming their parents. I suggested that parental behavior may cause a child to feel wounded.

On Sunday, I went to the Catholic liturgy. The reading from Hebrews 11 on faith was a good one. How much we follow in the footsteps of others! We are saved by grace, but we receive salvation by faith. We do not receive all of God's promises, but enough to recognize them from afar and to know when they have been fulfilled.

Luke 12, a passage on discipleship, encourages us to travel light, to be prepared for the mystery of God's coming—the sacrament of the moment—and to let go of the past and the future. The present is all we need to live with intensity. Yet I find my meditation on the past to be healing and joyful. I seem to need a balance of past, present, and future. I am grateful that I can live in the present, looking to the past and also to the future. Yet Luke's counsel not to miss the present is good. I want to pay attention to my life here in prison and to the other inmates.

I received a wonderful gift: Manny has been gracious to me. After his disdain came greetings and a smile.

> WE DO NOT RECEIVE ALL OF GOD'S PROMISES, BUT ENOUGH TO RECOGNIZE THEM FROM AFAR AND TO KNOW WHEN THEY HAVE BEEN FULFILLED.

Wednesday, August 11

Dick leaves prison this morning for South Carolina, where he will do roofing. I think he will make it, though he does not have a clear goal for his life. I'm concerned that he may become bored and revert to alcohol. I pray God's blessings upon him.

This morning, I felt confused and stressed, internal pressure that seems to say I am not okay. Bonhoeffer was such an able public figure. Although I seem to others to be strong, dedicated, and thoughtful, I am more modest and indecisive. But I am who I am.

You know, O God, that I struggle to keep going and that I wonder about life's meaning.

A letter to fellow prisoners of conscience

I remember each of you with appreciation and gratitude. The reality of a community shaped by a passion for justice and love both inspires and encourages me. Thank you. I remember you in my prayers, as I am sure many of you pray for me.

I will be released October 1. I look forward to moving from confinement to freedom. Yet I want to remain present here in the meantime. I have things to learn about inmates, the prison system, myself, and the nature of my calling both now and when I am released. I know that I will remain involved in the global war against the poor and that other foci for my energy will emerge.

I regret that we did not obtain 150 cosponsors for House Bill 1258, but we made an impact. The bill remains an important arrow in our quiver; people responded to our call for investigation. However, the Congress seems bent on avoiding investigation of atrocities in Iraq as well as in Latin America. Our policies of domination are operating in Venezuela, Haiti, and Colombia. We have much to chew on!

—⚏—

I rejoice in how God has led me to care about the other inmates and to seek right relationships with them. I find some of my relationships expanding and deepening a bit, though most are still limited.

Larry has taken a special interest in me, telling me some of what it means for him to be a Muslim. He does not want to be identified with Elijah Muhammad, the American activist and leader of the Black Muslims (1934–1975). Larry is a Muslim who happens to be black. I enjoy his friendship and our conversations. I make popcorn for him; he shares with me a special dish he makes from noodles, meats, and salad. As we pass on the sidewalk or in the dorm, he always asks, "How's it going, Mr. B?"

> I REJOICE IN HOW GOD HAS LED ME TO CARE ABOUT THE OTHER INMATES AND TO SEEK RIGHT RELATIONSHIPS WITH THEM.

Thursday, August 12

I awoke in the night deeply anguished about our nation. Our move toward totalitarianism is frightening, not so much for me as for my children and my grandchildren. So I got up and read the latest edition of *The Nation*, which discusses the problems of securing a fair election. Recounts and election inequities are indications of the erosion of democracy by the people and the onset of democracy for economic elites. I read about the Latinization of the United States, which seems evident, and an article about Colombia. Paramilitary groups are deeply entrenched in Colombia's power structure, and beneath the violence lies a culture of terror whose principal arm is unemployment. My morning readings gave me a bit of hope, not in people but in God, who works in ways we cannot see or know.[3]

Thank you, O God, Lord of life and our final hope.

I puzzle about my public witness. My life of solitude remains strong and a reason for rejoicing. My interpersonal life with Judy, family, and friends is strong. My witness in the public arena has been focused on SOA/WHINSEC and the activities of its graduates. But it is only a small part of our nation's militarism. Perhaps I need to consider work beyond the SOA/WHINSEC. I can make a solid witness on various issues. War and patriotism have taken so many lives and resources. I try to influence my congressional representative; my senators are timid in this area.

From politics to resistance—is that still my call?

Sunday, August 15

This morning was a joy, and then I languished. I am tired and confused, but I read the Bonhoeffer biography.[4] Eventually I just enjoyed a beautiful day. I finished getting all my letters in the mail. Writing letters is a task I enjoy.

Tony was up on the hill and tried to engage me in conversation, as did Ted. I was not up for conversation, so I left. I pray for Ted and for Tony, who is centered in his dreams and visions and writing about them.

I read some Emily Dickinson:

A death-blow is a life-blow to some
Who, till they died, did not alive become;
Who, had they lived, had died, but when
They died, vitality begun.[5]

At 11:40 a.m. there was a call for an emergency count. We returned to our cubicles wondering what had happened. Someone escaped, we thought.

I began to reread *The Power and the Glory*, by Graham Greene.[6] It is the story of a priest who is tortured by alcohol and fear, the tale of the struggle of a ravaged soul.

We waited. I lay down to read, think, and relax. People stood on tiptoes looking over the five-foot walls, trying to see what was happening. It grew quiet. We thought the guards were coming. But they didn't come, and conversation resumed as people talked across the walls from cube to cube.

At 12:45 p.m. five officers came down the hall and stood across from my cubicle. They interrogated Merrill, an able young man, a fine basketball player, and a Messianic Christian. Then they put handcuffs on him and took him out. His roommate didn't know why they took him away. Was there a snitch?

At 1:40 another count was called for. We waited. What was going on?

At 1:46 someone said, "They are coming in." Quiet again. Nobody came.

At 2:50 people are being interviewed in the TV room. My time will come.

At 3:15 I am summoned to the TV room and asked: Did you see a gun? Were you aware of a situation in which a gun would be needed? Would you report it if you saw a gun?

At 4:30 there was a standing count.

At 5:00 we ate supper.

Wednesday, August 18

A letter to my children

I have been thinking about you in recent days, giving thanks for each of you and how well your lives keep unfolding, though I know there are struggles and challenges along the way.

Each of you is special to me. I sit here looking at family pictures. You each have a special smile and character. I read each morning from Martha Hickman's book *Healing after Loss*.[7] One particular reading, where she quotes Dag Hammarskjöld, reminded me of you: "In the point of rest at the center of our being, we encounter a world where all things are at rest in the same way. Then a tree becomes a mystery, a cloud a revelation, each man [and woman] a cosmos of whose riches we can only catch glimpses."[8]

Glimpses of you, your spouses, and your children have the same power for me. What a gift I find in our family! Thank you, miracles all.

Judy Pilgrim was here yesterday, and our relationship continues to unfold. Another gift! I am still grateful for the forty-nine years Joyce and I had together. The God of life is good, when we can see the good. As my friend Bill Coffin says, there is no shortage of miracles, only those who cannot see them.

Dad

P.S. I get out at 8:30 on October 1—not long!!!

—⁂—

Max, a Baptist minister, and I discussed gay and lesbian unions. He sees them as a slippery slope. Once marriage is no longer the norm, he wonders, what happens next—polygamy? Max said that we humans seem intrinsically heterosexual. However, there are historical variations of this relationship. Celibacy, chosen by some, is not a threat to marriage as normative. For me, gay relationships are not either. In our culture, patriarchy, male domination, seems to be operative. Men want to control both women and other men who deviate from the norm. The demeaning of women here troubles me, as does male domination in general. It seems to me that war is a male phenomenon.

Thursday, August 19

I have completed Bonhoeffer's biography and want to review it in a few days to identify major themes and insights. It affected me; I don't yet know how.

Saturday, August 21

Yesterday Bill, Kathryn, Gene, and Penny came to visit, along with Judy. It was a rich day. I talked with them individually as well as together; and we shared the Lord's Supper, which Bill led.

Sunday, August 22

The Catholic liturgy today was helpful in dealing with the question of salvation. "Some are last who will be first, and some are first who will be last" (Luke 13:30) is a difficult saying. If salvation means healing and not an ultimate decision, it would be clear. Who can be healed?

The sermon focused on boats as a metaphor for our lives in the Spirit: tugboats, which are always on the job; sailboats, which move in a good wind; and rafts, which go with the current. The talk of boats made me think of Grandfather Moe, captain of a tugboat on Lake Superior. "People will come from east and west, from north and south" (Luke 13:29). I'd like to consider more how the wind of the Spirit moves us.

Monday, August 23

A reflection on confinement as a gift

I have been confined for over four months now. The prison keeps track of me with midnight counts, stand-up counts, state-your-number counts. I am confined in every sense of the word. Separation, enclosure, isolation, and withdrawal to a desert have all been disciplines in my life of faith. Confinement in prison adds another dimension.

Flannery O'Connor had lupus, a debilitating disease that sapped her energy and confined her to a farm in Georgia. Her affliction and confinement were chronic. She borrowed a phrase from Teilhard de Chardin, "passive diminishment," to describe the quality of accepting with grace any affliction or loss that can't be changed. And she saw the good in diminishment. "I can with one eye squinted take it all as a blessing," she wrote.[9] Confinement led her to use her energy attending to life at the farm and to the people around her.

I consider how to be more present to life today. What I pay attention to sharpens my life. If I pay attention to what is in the future, I may miss something now. What about this day and this time? Much of the inmates' energy is focused outside on appeals, family matters, girlfriends. Mostly they focus their energy on getting out of prison. They see life in the future.

I reflect on my time here. I have paid attention to building relationships with inmates and to finding space for others in my heart. I also have paid attention to myself, to my dispositions, tiredness, and confusion. I give thanks for my friends, colleagues, and family, and cherish their support. I am especially grateful now for the women in my life. I think about those giving and receiving support in the Living Room, those caring for Penuel Ridge, and those working for the people in Nashville. I am concerned about the graduates of SOA/WHINSEC and how they affect the people and communities in Latin America. I see how atrocities take shape in Iraq and in Latin America and how investigations into violence and torture are avoided, rejected, and ignored. I laud the people of God who gather in praise, service, love, and hope. I consider the beauty of flowers, sky, running water, and peaches for breakfast.

Confinement has provided me with unwanted isolation, but it also has brought me to the deeper meanings that lie quietly in my present life. I listen better and let events be my teacher.

Even in prison, I have found holy presence, filling life with sacredness. Such a gift! Vincent van Gogh said, "I think that everything that is really good and beautiful . . . comes from God."[10] I think of this observation especially in the morning and at night when I retire. I am grateful to be able to reflect theologically on the incredible life given to me. There is majesty in all things.

Flannery O'Connor wrote that Catholic writers, like herself, "will feel life from the standpoint of the central Christian mystery: that it has, for all its horror, been found by God to be worth dying for."[11] Such a wondrous way to see!

Paul, a prisoner, wrote to the people of God in Philippi,

> I rejoice in the Lord greatly. . . . I have learned to be content with whatever I have. I know what it is to have little, and I know what it is to have plenty. In any and all circumstances I have learned the secret of being well-fed and of going hungry, of having plenty and of being in need. I can do all things through him who strengthens me. In any case, it was kind of you to share my distress. (Phil. 4:10-14)

Tuesday, August 24

Another day! Thank you. How important it is for me to say thank you to the Holy One, the Eternal God who grounds my life in a greater reality!

Today was an excellent time for reflection. Exercise was good, as was breakfast. I tried several times to see my counselor about commissary care and finally saw him about 5:30 p.m. I read some of *Hard Time Blues*, a book on the prison system written by Sasha Abramsky.[12] I mailed another set of cards and letters. I had a lengthy conversation with Saxter and called Bill Barnes.

This evening I became upset as I thought about Rep. Cooper's lack of response to House Bill 1258. There will be no audit for military expenditures, no consternation, no fight—at this point, it feels like a lost cause for the SOA Watch.

Wednesday, August 25

Yesterday I was tired and languishing again—doing my work, eating, exercising, passing time, but not energized enough to read or write. Today I rested and feel renewed.

Thank you, O Creator, Redeemer, spirit of life and breath.

—ɱ—

My review of Hard Time Blues *by Sasha Abramsky*

Hard Time Blues tells the story of how politics built the U.S. prison system. The author explores what is "part of the American experience that also represents something darker, more untamed and brutal that exists within the human psyche."

The darker side takes form in the United States' having the largest · prison system in the world. It is larger than the Russian and Chinese gulags; its population exceeds the number of people imprisoned under apartheid in South Africa thirty years ago. We make up 5 percent of the world's population, yet we comprise 20 percent of the world's prison population. England, with a population of 69 million, has only 60,000 in prison. In 1980, the United States had 300,000 people in prison; now that number is more than two million. Why is that?

Crime reports in the media each night make people afraid, especially of those who are poor and marginalized; so we seek candidates who are tough on crime. Political rhetoric attempts to incite cynicism and fear; politicians stop talking about hope and inclusion. Massive imprisonment has become the national will because people are afraid. In addition, privatization of prisons has made them one of the most profitable businesses around; it is profitable to keep people in prison as long as possible.

Abramsky provides a telling analysis of how California governor Pete Wilson used crime as a major platform in his bid for election. Crime and punishment dominated the news, as it still does; and this hot-button issue was the key to his election. As governor, he kept his promise to secure three-strikes legislation, which is now replicated in many states. Prison construction followed. Later, Gray Davis used this theme in his election campaign, and more prisons were built. California has over 160,000 people in prisons.

The criminalization of drugs, which is seen as a social issue requiring rehabilitation in many countries, stands as the major reason for the increased number of people in prison. Mandatory sentencing laws, arrests on conspiracy charges, and minimum sentencing for drug crimes have put more and more persons in prison.

The author, who has written for the *New York Times* and the *Village Voice*, says that the United States deals with complex social problems by locking people up, which gets them out of the way. In Nashville and Atlanta, we get homeless people out of sight in various ways. Panhandling ordinances are easy to enforce, so homeless people are put in prison too.

Abramsky tells the story of Billy Ochoa, a man whose petty crimes supported his drug habit. He secured funds through welfare fraud. After three offenses, he was sentenced to 326 years in prison for committing $2,100 worth of welfare fraud. Has the justice system gone crazy? The cost of punishment escalates year by year, leaving social needs for health care, education, training, and rehabilitation without funds.

A society fails when a significant percentage of the people imprisoned have committed crimes because legitimate jobs are unavailable. In the federal prison in Manchester, Kentucky, most of the five hundred men in the minimum security facility are incarcerated because they wanted or needed money. They committed nonviolent crimes. Many could not find jobs that paid a living wage.

What should be done? Investment in education remains a major need. So does the creation of jobs that pay a living wage: enough money for housing, food, transportation, and clothing. Adequate payment is needed for people who are injured on the job and cannot work. We need to distinguish more clearly those who commit violent crimes from those whose crimes are nonviolent. Means of punishment other than imprisonment are available. Finally, we need better control of guns that facilitate crime.

A massive prison system built for political gain and without public debate stands as a great tragedy in our nation's history, costly both in taxes and in the destruction of families and lives.

Saturday, August 28

I am feeling alienated from the values that are so dominant among the inmates. Yet their values are the same as those of our culture. Many have used illegal means to get money. Halliburton seems to do the same thing without reprisal—a slap on the hand, but no penalty. I am so sick of our system of injustice.

I am unclear about my priorities. I miss being with Judy. I am tired, both physically and mentally. I feel confused, alienated. I am not depressed, however; and I do not despair. I'll come through. But I do not enjoy the time. Why my lack of energy? I am unable to fulfill emotions that arise, so they become dormant. Die? I think not.

Monday, August 30

August is nearly over. Only thirty days in September, and I will be released. I do not feel captive, but here of my own choice; so in many ways I am already free.

How grateful I am for you, God, whose presence transcends human boundaries: fences, walls, guards, counts!

Tuesday, August 31

I awoke early and thought about my release on October 1. I wrote a note about my thoughts:

Prayer involves trust and wonder. As a young Helen Keller said, "God is in me as the sun is in the color and fragrance of a flower—the Light in my darkness, the Voice in my silence."[13]

[7]
SEPTEMBER: LEAVING PRISON

Integral salvation is not posthistorical. It is realized in a liberation
process that involves moments of conflict. All historical liberation, even
the liberation brought to us by Jesus Christ, occurs in the context of a
covenant of suffering, pain, and death between human beings and God.
Suffering is the price we have to pay for the resistance the fatalizing sys-
tems put up to each and every quantum leap in history.

—LEONARDO BOFF

Wednesday, September 1, 2004

I am unfocused and have little energy for more than puttering around. I cope, for which I am grateful. I may be suffering from modest depression; but it seems like a normal down, which will be followed by an up.

"This is the day that the LORD has made; let us rejoice and be glad in it" (Ps. 118:24). This is a good word for me. Stop languishing; see the day, this day, as the Lord's day; and rejoice!

How difficult it must be for Red to rejoice in this day! He is twenty-nine and has been here for ten years.

Jesus comes to us disguised in the midst of the people, hidden among the poor, the sick, the prisoners, the strangers. *Help me, O God, to see Jesus.*

Love is of God. Wherever love is, God's grace is present also. Are people here shaped, warped, destroyed so that they cannot connect in loving ways with other persons?

Are people here saying no to laws that beat them down? All tyrannies are based on contempt for human beings. God chose to be incarnate as a poor man, a worker, a Jew. He was the victim of the law—used to beat him down—and contempt. Jesus was human like us, and he loved us.

Thursday, September 2

I have written a letter to Simon about our altercation yesterday. What was it about—noise? Writing the letter was helpful to me, though I have no idea what his response will be.

A letter to Simon, an inmate across the aisle

I am sitting here thinking about our altercation yesterday. It is important that I learn what I can from the experience, since I do try to keep growing as a person—a person of faith, a citizen, a friend, and at this time in my life, a prisoner. It is not easy for me here, as you know. I make many mistakes, and I appreciate you and others who try to keep me on track. I am aware of your help and kindness. Thank you.

Before I retired in 1996, I had the discipline of work for fifty years. I had the discipline and the joy of being a husband for forty-nine years and of being a father of six children. I state all this, not to be impressive, but to say that over the years, I developed ways of doing things, ways that I found most helpful and that helped me to survive. These patterns were familiar to me and gave my life structure and purpose.

But with discipline comes a certain rigidity. I wanted to keep living as I had been, and I tried to do so here. For instance, my desk at home is usually cluttered. I organize it repeatedly, but it always gets cluttered again. That pattern did not work here. It took me a long time to understand the rule about keeping your desk clean. There are so many rules.

All along, the love I found among the community of inmates was absolutely essential to surviving and getting along here. You and others have taught me. I do appreciate it! I hope you know that.

But I resisted. I wanted to act as I had before, to make the place where I lived comfortable for me. I'm sure you feel that way as well. We make over our cubes into places that are enjoyable, and we do things we enjoy.

Somewhere along the line, I learned that one goal here is to survive. Several inmates said that survival was their primary goal. Eventually, I saw what they meant, and I have acted in ways so I could survive. I set aside time for silence and exercise; I learned the rules, and I followed them.

I heard you say yesterday that my patterns are outmoded, old-fashioned, and inappropriate. You have tried to help me along the way, only to find that I rejected your input. You looked out for me, and then I was not appreciative! I argued with you. I asserted myself in ways that seemed to you that I knew it all. (Is that what you were feeling and thinking?) I argued with your suggestions; I didn't just accept them. This was difficult for you, I suppose. Our conflict was centered at the intersection of your awareness of what I needed to do and my resistance to changing my long-developed patterns, which have helped me survive outside the walls.

Do I understand accurately? I want to understand. I think what you were saying was important for me to hear.

I do have trouble with the way you speak to me, which feels condescending and at times arrogant and rude. But our life histories are different, and our histories shape our behavior. For instance, some people enjoy speaking loudly to each other, cursing each other, shouting across the dorm; but it is foreign to me. I can't participate even when I try. And I have tried, but as you say, I just don't get it.

I would like to have a conversation about all this; but we have different ways of talking, and I'm not sure we could do so. So I have chosen to write this letter.

I want you to know that I think highly of you, and I appreciate the ways you have looked out for me even though I have had difficulty accepting your help. You have expressed goodwill to me. Thank you.

Friday, September 3

Simon has said nothing about my letter. I'll wait. If he does not respond, we will not have a relationship. *Bless his life, O God. Bless Don and Larry and Steve.*

I am discouraged by our national consensus. Everything I care about in public life—health care, housing for the homeless, low-income housing, living wages, development of resources, education—has eroded. Instead our nation focuses on fear, security, and military solutions. Nonviolent resistance is needed.

Saturday, September 4

Last night, not far from from my cubicle, there was a lot of loud arguing near the microwave. I was upset and could not sleep because of the shouting. I devised several possible ways to deal with the constant commotion in that area: break the microwave? hide it? cut the cord? Gerry suggested I try earplugs. He gave me a set, and they worked.

Labor Day, September 6

My relationship with the inmates is now more complex than before. I have made overtures to several but have had no response. My relationship with Red continues to puzzle me. I like Larry, who always is friendly to me. Brent and I have in-depth conversations. I have a host of enjoyable, casual relationships with other inmates. The guards seem friendlier and less arrogant. I actually enjoy them in some ways. They maintain order among the inmates, which is not easy. Anger can lead to arguments, fights, and acts of hostility. Since inmates are not allowed to express anger without reprisal by the system, unresolved anger festers, leading to emotional confusion and depression.

Tuesday, September 7

I realized this morning that only one or two people here have made an effort to know me and to find out why I am here. Almost all of my other relationships consist of bantering and functional conversations about needs, work, concerns, games, and sports.

I had hoped to get to know Red, but he has little interest in me.

My bulletin board provides me with an opportunity to tell a bit about my family and about people of faith. I feel sad that I cannot tell more. Life here is so superficial. When I have tried to move toward deeper relationships, I have been ignored or slighted. Yet some people here, such as the musical group or the two men I see walking together, seem to be friends.

When Kerry's baby was born, we shared his happiness. Illness and death of loved ones provide similar occasions to connect emotionally. Crises bring us together for a moment, but then the separation returns. Privacy is necessary to feel safe.

To bless is to say good things. *God, bless all your creatures and make us a blessing to one another.*

Wednesday, September 8

It is 5:00 a.m., and the guards just went through for an inmate count.

Yesterday I submitted the names of the people who will be picking me up when I'm released—Philip and Judy—along with their license plate number and the style and color of their car.

Before that, I was summoned to the administration building. No one was there, so I knocked on the closed door. Officer Smathers went in, and I asked him whether I should wait. He said that they would come for me when they were ready.

I waited. Then I knocked again. I thought I heard the administrative assistant, Mrs. Bark, say to come in. But when I opened the door, she commanded, "Get out. Get out. Shut the door." I banged the door shut and left. Such anger is not acceptable; I expect to hear from someone about this incident. So it goes in prison, over and over again.

> PEACE IS NOT THE ABSENCE OF STRUGGLE BUT THE PRESENCE OF LOVE.

I felt disrespected, as usual, and angry. Disrespect for inmates is standard procedure. I talked with Pablo about my anger. "Tell people what goes on here," he said.

Peace is not the absence of struggle but the presence of love. How blessed I am! So many people of faith have crossed my path and enriched me. I think of my mother and father; Lydia; Mitzi; Ruth; Judi; Mark; Mrs. Richardson; Carl Lange; Huntley Dupre; Hugo Thompson; Mitau; Adams; Robert McAfee Brown and his wife; Reinhold Niebuhr; Parker Lansdale; Vic; Judy E.; Joyce (so much); my children; folks in Arkansas, Creston, Chicago, Nashville; Bill, Ken; Clarence, Proffitt; Basil and Evalee King; Bob King—so many, and many I have not met but about whom I've read. Such a pantheon! *Thank you, God.*

Bill Coffin says that we as a nation have separated freedom from virtue, so democracy languishes.[1] Yesterday while working, I temporarily left the cafeteria through a side door. An officer told me to go back in through the front door, but I did not hear him, and I went back in the side door. He came after me, pronto, but could not find me. Saxter and Ron laughed.

I asked Simon to describe me in one word. He answered, "*Irrelevant.*" To him, I live in a different world that has no relevance to him.

Thursday, September 9

Last night I was aware that I was depleted: spiritually empty, mentally weary, emotionally numb. I do believe, however. I know that God cares for me and my friends. I am not alone, and even here I feel the care and support of many people. I am grateful for acts of friendship, congeniality, and fun. So I feel drained, and yet I've started another day.

I puzzle about my strained relationship with Simon, who has been kind to me in several ways, and I to him. I want to reread my letter to him and see how I might try again to deepen our friendship. Relationships are difficult and demanding. I feel strain in my relationship with Red and Saxter.

All this I offer to you, O Comforter. Say the word so that I may be healed.

This morning a guard announced over the loudspeaker that the weight room will be closed until a week from tomorrow. We don't know why. Perhaps it is part of the guards' effort to bring order in response to the burning of a gay inmate's mattress, the smoking, the stealing. Later, I discover it is because an inmate was in the weight room without wearing proper shoes. The whole camp has been punished. I do not have steel-toed shoes, but I go to the weight room each morning to do my exercise routine. If I had been there when the guard came in, I too would have been punished.

For every rule or constraint, there is a corresponding testing of the limits of the rule. The whole camp is shot through with rules and

> FOR EVERY RULE OR CONSTRAINT, THERE IS A CORRESPONDING TESTING OF THE LIMITS OF THE RULE. THE WHOLE CAMP IS SHOT THROUGH WITH RULES AND THE INMATES' ATTEMPTS TO GET AROUND THEM.

the inmates' attempts to get around them. Inmates take food from the kitchen, smoke, and use the gym early in the morning—all in reaction to the rules.

Sunday, September 12

Yesterday Roy had an altercation with an officer and was put in the solitary housing unit, the hole. I pray for him and for the officer, who relishes being tough. He does bring some order.

I am aware that I am distancing myself emotionally from Cory, Steve, Al, and Dick. All my relationships with the other inmates seem difficult, and I will not be here long enough to work through them. So I move on, but I experience a loss.

Monday, September 13

A letter to family and friends

I have a few more weeks left in the federal prison in Manchester. The time has moved along, and soon—on October 1, to be exact—I will be free from confinement. I am looking forward to seeing some of you at Penuel Ridge's twentieth anniversary banquet on October 12.

I CONTINUE TO BELIEVE THAT PRISONS ARE OBSOLETE AS A WAY TO BRING ORDER TO OUR SOCIETY.

The middle period of time here has been easier for me, especially since I have had a cubicle, a light, a desk, a locker for storage, and a chair. I also know the rules better, so I rest more easily within the system. I have not had an altercation for two weeks. Alleluia!

I continue to believe that prisons are obsolete as a way to bring order to our society. Violent people, of course, need safe spaces to protect them and others. However, the five hundred people in this camp do not need to be here. They need to be with their families, at their jobs, and within the communities that support them.

As you know, I am part of the effort to close SOA/WHINSEC, the U.S. Army school in Columbus, Georgia, because of serious human rights violations, including torture and assassinations, by graduates of the school. Congress does not support serious investigation into the military policies that led to these atrocities—a sad commentary on our democracy.

Furthermore, those who dissent from government policies are labeled as troublemakers, and the cost of their dissent increases. Three instances come to mind:

- When I was arrested, my bond was set at $1,000, twice as much as my previous arrest.
- The twenty-seven people arrested for trespassing on the base were upright, responsible citizens and could have been released on their own recognizance, but the judge denied us this possibility.
- Sixteen of the twenty-seven people were given the maximum sentence of six months. Ten received three months. Most everyone was fined.

In an article in *The Nation*, August 16/23, 2004, Jim Hightower says the Bush administration is "using federal, state and local police to conduct an undeclared war against dissent, literally incarcerating Americans who publicly express their disagreements with [them] and [their] policies. . . . If incarceration is not enough to deter dissenters, how about some old-fashioned goonsquad tactics like infiltration and intimidation of protestors?"[2]

We are seeing a doctrine of permanent war and a new policy of keeping dissenters far from the president. We no longer think of peace, yet we are called to be peacemakers. As Pope Paul VI wrote in 1967, "Development is the new name for peace."[3] We must recover a vision and a hope of peace.

The cost of dissent goes up, but so do the reasons for dissent. The notion of perpetual war to fight terrorism is gaining credence. Violence and war are thought to be the only way to ensure the nation's security, and national security is used to justify all kinds of military policies, including interrogation and torture. Dissent becomes essential to choosing life over death.

We are called to be peacemakers. We must stand up for peace, lest we forget God's promise of shalom. "Blessed are the peacemakers," says Jesus. And so we shall continue.

Grace and peace,

Don

Tuesday, September 14

Confinement as a problem: distortion, brokenness, injustice, and sin

I recently wrote about confinement as a gift. Confinement has given me an extended period of time to stand apart and look more deeply at my personal, interpersonal, and public life.

Confinement also is a problem, and that has become clearer to me the longer I have been here. I have seen how it affects me and others, including the guards and staff.

While I have learned to deal with solitude and silence in productive ways, I also have had problems with mild depression, lows that string out over time and make life distressing. However, I have not had any serious depression, even without the medication I took before being incarcerated. I experience stress and confusion that are disorienting. This seems to have increased as I approach the end of my time here.

Confinement has affected me at a deeper level. While times of solitude, prayer, meditation, writing, and reflection have made me feel alive, I have also felt emotionally disconnected, numb, empty, and alone.

I am often shattered by the form of conversation here; though there are moments of laughter, the talk is more often brutal, loud, argumentative, and hostile. Kindness and joy, which I value, are not fostered by prison culture.

I am a bit of a loner. I enjoy walking alone, looking at clouds and trees, feeling the wind. Others share my love of nature. Several enjoy finding insects to feed to the frogs in the pond. This is perhaps a level of kindness.

My values differ from the values of most people here. Tattoos and upper-body strength are valued, as is being a star at football, softball, or basketball. All these are symbols of strength and power.

There is patriarchy-with-a-passion here. I hear it in the way men address their wives over the phone. Their words are often spoken with brutal condemnation and only at times with gentleness, wonder, and joy. This troubles me.

I have found only two men with whom I share some political agreement, though not on matters of race. I play cribbage and discuss the Bible with another person who has a rather fundamentalist understanding of scripture. We enjoy the game.

Most of the people here see no connection between freedom and virtue.

Some are libertarian. Wanting to avoid all restrictions on their lives, they resist rules and institutions. The exaltation of freedom gives them little sense of community. My struggle has been to connect freedom and virtue. I am free, but my aim is to love God, my neighbor, myself, and the earth. Freedom and virtue intersect.

> There's a wideness in God's mercy like the wideness of the sea;
> there's a kindness in God's justice, which is more than liberty.[4]

Thursday, September 16

In the evening, I watched a movie, but I did not enjoy it. I feel emotionally numb. My time here has become more difficult. I am unfocused and less aware of my foundational commitments. I am surviving, which I guess is good. How wearisome to have been here for such a long time! In an environment of punishment, incarceration, repression, and erratic uses of power, human life cannot prosper. The resources that help me cope—the weight room, the use of the gymnasium—keep being withdrawn.

Yesterday an inmate who is about fifty said that the younger men here are new at living with others and don't understand the constraints of community, so they act like teenagers. That seems true. They enjoy themselves, but in unconstructive ways. Their relationships are shallow, characterized by macho language and talk about sex, drugs, money, women, cars, and bodybuilding.

I have been able to communicate with them at times and have earned their respect, but not their admiration or their interest in my life and values. I have pride in my life, which can be a problem for me and for others.

Sunday, September 19

The prison world seems beyond my understanding. I am reminded of the story I heard while I was in Colombia about people who came to visit that country. Those who came for two weeks wrote a book. Those who stayed six months wrote an article. Those who stayed a year or two wrote nothing.

The grandiosity of life is apparent to me. The only things I feel certain about are the value of seeing the world from the perspective of the oppressed and the poor, a belief that God is in the midst of all things, an awareness of the evil that human beings do, and a sense of beauty. I give thanks for the beauty in people, in Judy, in the sky, in children. I feel that the beauty of God's creation is threatened; and I shudder not for myself, but for my children, my grandchildren, and all the children of the world.

I have just returned from breakfast, exercise, and tai chi. The morning is cold. I cannot use the weights since I don't have steel-toed shoes. I went to the gym and was unsure about being there. I was told that I could be there, but some people say that the gym is closed to visits until the lights come on. Officers enforce the rules differently and arbitrarily. The inmates are in a constant state of uneasiness because of this.

Monday, September 20

My new roommate, Bart, has settled in.

The New York Times sits here, filled with data; yet I resist reading it. Why? In many ways, I do not enjoy public life. It is too much to grasp and requires a response. Yet I keep reading about it, cutting out articles to read later while I wait for work or for the counts.

Tuesday, September 21

I use the word *languish* to describe my current physical, emotional, mental, and spiritual condition. To languish means "to be or live in a state of depression or decreasing vitality."[5] I am sad, but not hopelessly so. Change has

I AM SAD, BUT NOT HOPELESSLY SO.

been the main cause of my languishing. The rules have changed so that people here have little time during the day to rest and read. I go to the dining room at 11:30 a.m. for work—earlier if I want to eat lunch—and I stay until the evening meal is completed and the cleanup is done.

I have tried to befriend Red, a twenty-nine-year-old who has been in prison for ten years. We have bantered and joked a bit, but my efforts mostly have been in vain. Cory says that Red loves me, that I am special to him. But he only shows it with filthy language, which does not communicate to me. So I wonder. I would like to give up the effort but will keep at it.

With a new roommate, I have had to reorganize my cubicle and figure out where to put my stuff again. I have given Bart half of the bulletin board, and he has posted pictures of his wife, his son, a nice car and house, and himself in sweatpants looking cool.

I joyfully anticipate my release. But then I will have to deal with a homecoming, time with others on October 3, and an anniversary celebration at Penuel Ridge on October 12. I don't know whether I have enough energy to cope with all that. This loss of vigor, this sadness, this listlessness feels strange.

My effort to get some packing boxes has also been upsetting. I need them to prepare to leave, but Mr. Markham will not allow me to keep boxes in my room. Just another problem! Part of my languishing is due to the constant feeling that I am doing something that violates the rules, that I might be reprimanded or put in the solitary housing unit. Most everything I do could violate the rules, so I worry: Do I have the right clothes and shoes? Do I need a hat or not? Is my desk cleaned up? Have I cleaned under the bed and desk? Are my cabinets dusted? Is the floor clean? The worry is constant.

Trying to order my life, my world, and my thoughts is a challenge at almost every point. The world I order becomes disordered again. The challenge feels Sisyphean, like pushing a rock up the same hill over and over again. I have lived long enough to know that my energy will come back. I live by faith that I will be invigorated by energy other than my own.

At breakfast I always get one slice of toast. This morning there was no toast. I looked a bit startled, then sad, and slowly turned around to get some sugarcoated cereal instead.

As I started to leave, Kerry said, "I'll make you a piece of toast."

"That would be great," I said.

He brought the toast to my table when it was done—an act of kindness, a rare event.

Wednesday, September 22

I have had two breakthroughs in relationships. Red and I connected, though not on a deep level. He is shaped by his time in prison; I am not a factor in his life.

I talked to Simon about my irrelevance. He said his words were in jest.

Much of life in prison is shaped by the need not to reveal oneself, to beware of snitches or threats, to be tough so as not to be threatened. The violence in prison is created in part by inmates but also by the prison's structure, which relies on power and threat to maintain order. Disrespect creates more disrespect. Anger, which provokes actions that are seen as threatening, results in greater reliance on orders, rules, and threats.

We live in a world of escalating violence. As a nation, we cope with violence against us by retaliating with greater violence. Our national resources are devoted to military solutions. We do not focus on building up life, much less our common life. We support violent solutions in the Middle East, including, for example, our long support of military solutions in response to the Palestinians; but we act without sufficient recognition of how violence breeds violence. Most of our foreign aid is military aid, or it is controlled by military objectives. Aid is given according to our national self-interest, and the result of increasing militarism is a violent world. Because our military is strong, terror is the means we choose to secure change.

My witness seems so small. O Lord, you have so much more power and resources than does our nation. I pray that we can learn again the ways of peace, negotiation, compromise, accommodation, and creative solutions to injustice.

Thursday, September 23

I was in the bathroom at 4:00 a.m., preparing for the day. Gerry and Jack were brought in by the guards for urine tests for drugs—so early in the morning!

Today I reflected on preemptive violence and how it is used to justify war. Of course, we must resist evil, but war should be our last choice, if a choice at all. We must learn nonviolent ways of dealing with injustice.

Friday, September 24

I awoke at 3:40 a.m., thinking of what I might say to the people who will gather to welcome me home. Ideas popped into my head as I lay in my bunk, but I did not want to turn on what one inmate calls "Beisswenger's airport light"! Instead, I went into the bathroom and made a few notes.

What has helped me to survive? The inmates, connections with other people, and kindness. I have also been helped by thinking about the meaning and impact of my time here. Basically, I consider the time an offering to God. I do not yet know its importance.

Jim, who is about thirty-eight, came into the bathroom. He lived across from me at the beginning of my incarceration. He said he had read all night. I told him what I was doing. He said he recalled when I came to the camp. I didn't know anybody; and all the shouting, hollering, and cussing seemed to confuse me. "Inmates are crude," he said, "but you are different."

Saturday, September 25

1:15 a.m.: Guards come by for a stand-up count.

2:15 a.m.: Another stand-up count. The lights come on suddenly. Sixty men in Skivvies stand in their doorways to state their names and numbers.

2:28 a.m.: A police car arrives; its lights swirl through the camp. The police found an inmate walking around upstairs. He was sent to the solitary housing unit.

7:15 a.m.: Breakfast.

I see my life as a Spirit-filled journey, shaped by Jesus and abiding in the love of a holy God, who takes away sin and distortion, who is just and seeks to redeem the world.

Sunday, September 26

I go on trying to live in God's presence, yet I am aware of my duplicity, my mixed motives, my struggles. There is so much beauty, peace, love, and truth in our lives. At times we must become as children again.

The piles of stuff on my desk, in my locker, and on the pillow trouble me. Even after I've been punished for this, organization still remains an issue for me. I feel guilty that I cannot do my writing. To understand, to learn—and to keep things available when I need them—is a great frustration.

Monday, September 27

When I am released, people will expect from me a witness: a word of hope, courage, and wisdom. Yet I am fragile and limited in understanding. So I offer my life and my gifts to God for this day and for the days ahead.

Into your hands, I commend my spirit. Give me joy, gladness, confidence, and grace to serve you.

So much is at stake. What I honor and value, my community in the outside world also values. My public concerns are also theirs. *O Lord, God, guide me through all the haze into the light of your love, truth, grace.*

I reflect on the Penuel Ridge community, the shape of its life and work, and its link with the poor. Penuel Ridge provides a center that honors both the Jewish and the Christian contemplative traditions. Because Jesus welcomed all people, Penuel Ridge welcomes all to rest in God's all-embracing love.

Tuesday, September 28

I was up last night writing about my conversations with Red and Simon. The inmates' lack of interest in other people here is striking. Few people have asked why I am here. All this makes me sad. People avoid connecting with others because they are afraid and need to protect themselves. They try to control their lives by trivialization; their goal is to pass time.

Wednesday, September 29

Two more nights, and I will be released. What a time to ponder! Yesterday I talked to Mr. Jobe, my caseworker, and clarified several things regarding my departure. He gave me permission to pack today. I did that, and I feel good about getting my things into two boxes and in moderately good order.

I still wonder about how to deal with the expectations of others upon my release. I think I should know more, be more profound.

O Lord, Holy Spirit, breathe in me on this new day. Help me to serve you with joy.

Today I will exercise, eat breakfast, participate in the Native American sweat lodge, pack a bit more, work on what I will say on Sunday, call Judy and Philip. What shall I leave here? *Guide me in this matter, O God.*

Stack said, "You're leaving Friday! You've had an impact on a lot of folks. They listen to you even if they don't show it, especially the young blacks."

Eb said, "You're the only white who has related to blacks here and earned their trust. Most whites talk a good game, but then they say racist stuff behind people's backs. I really thank you."

Talking about Red, Eb continued, "A lot of important things are going on for him. He's been here a long time—since he was nineteen—but you got to him, man. He'll never forget it. You reached out to him, and he knows it. He blocked me all the time. Someone had to reach him. Lots of people never had anyone reach them. Lots of people got something from knowing you."

—⟋⟍⟍—

News release from the Nashville Peace and Justice Center

On Friday, October 1, the Reverend Don Beisswenger, Vanderbilt Divinity School professor emeritus, will be released from the Federal Correctional Institution in Manchester, Kentucky, where he has been serving a six-month sentence for civil disobedience at the School of the Americas in November, 2003.

Before he goes home to rest and recover, he will make a short appearance at the Nashville Peace and Justice Center to greet supporters, old friends, and coworkers.

On the evening before, Thursday, September 30, the founder of the School of the Americas Watch, Father Roy Bourgeois, will speak in Benton Chapel at the Divinity School. His talk, "Terrorizing the Poor: U. S. Foreign Policy in Latin America," will address some of the hard questions he has had to grapple with in his life journey from Vietnam to Bolivia to the United States.

Open to the public, the lecture is sponsored by Vanderbilt Divinity School, the Center for Latin American and Iberian Studies, the Office of the University Chaplain and Affiliated Ministries, the Nashville Peace and Justice Center, and Latin American Solidarity Committee (LA CASA).

A reception will be held following the lecture.

On Sunday, October 3, Don Beisswenger and friends will hold a liturgy of celebration at Downtown Presbyterian Church. The Reverend Don Beisswenger, beloved pastor, advocate for the homeless, and Vanderbilt Divinity School professor emeritus, will join members of the Living Room (a weekly gathering of homeless and formerly homeless people that Beisswenger founded), Hillsboro Presbyterian Church, and the Nashville social justice community as they come together to welcome Don back from his six months in a federal penitentiary for civil disobedience.

The liturgy will celebrate Don's witness for justice on behalf of the victims of the School of the Americas. Don will be reading from his prison writings, and his supporters from all walks of life will be there to hear how Don plans to continue his witness for justice.

Beisswenger's six months in prison may seem a strange twist for a long, law-abiding life. However, Father Bourgeois' life, which inspired Beisswenger to make his decision to cross the line, has more turns than most. A Purple-Heart recipient, naval officer, priest, Bolivian social worker, and founder of the SOA Watch, Father Roy has made several radical shifts in his life. Born in Lutcher, Louisiana, he spent exactly four years in the Navy and exactly four years in federal prison for engaging in civil disobedience against the U.S. Army's School of the Americas, recently renamed Western Hemisphere Institute for Security Cooperation (WHINSEC).

In 1980, Father Roy became involved in issues surrounding U.S. foreign policy in El Salvador after four U.S. churchwomen, two of them friends, were raped and killed by Salvadoran soldiers trained and armed by the United States. An outspoken critic of U.S. foreign policy in Latin America, Father Roy founded the School of the Americas Watch in 1980. The SOA/WHINSEC, located at Fort Benning, Georgia, trains hundreds of soldiers from Latin America in combat skills, all paid for by U.S. taxpayers.

Roy has worked on and helped produce several documentary films, including *Gods of Metal* (1982) about the nuclear arms race and *School of Assassins* (1994). Both films received Academy Award nominations.

In 1997, Father Roy was the recipient of the 1997 Pax Christi U.S.A. Teacher of Peace Award. In December of 1998, he testified in Madrid before Spanish Judge Baltasar Garzon, seeking the extradition of Chile's ex-dictator General Augusto Pinochet.

Dozens of Nashvillians travel to Fort Benning every November to take part in the annual protest against the School of the Americas. Every year some people decide to cross the line from peaceful protest to civil disobedience. In 2003, Beisswenger joined the large numbers of people who have been arrested and sentenced for their actions at SOA/WHINSEC.

Both Beisswenger and Bourgeois hope that 2004 will see more people in the United States—and Nashville, in particular—become so passionate about justice that they will put their freedom on the line as well. The next protest at the gates of SOA/WHINSEC will be November 19–21.

Thursday, September 30

The opposite of love is not hate but fear.

What wonderful gifts you give, O Lord, through your servants who bless me each morning! The pilgrim journey is blessed by people here as well, by Henry, Red, and others. Bless the day as I do the merry-go-round, the purpose of which is unclear to me. May I be open to the spirit of this day and live to your honor and glory!

I went around getting signatures from people in the medical offices, the laundry, and the dining hall, as well as from the officer in charge. I did my exercises after breakfast and was afraid that Officer Mike would come in and make trouble for me even now that I am leaving. (I admit that he has been fair with me at points of conflict.) I got in a last game of spades. I helped clean up after lunch as a gift to the supervisor and the men who worked. I rested, took the green uniform back to the laundry, picked up my commissary report, and completed my packing. In the evening, I watched a bit of softball after taking a walk up the hill. I also viewed a video on the United States massacre of the Lakota Indians in 1890. We have been and still are a violent people.

—⁂—

My review and reflection on Angela Davis's Are Prisons Obsolete?[6]

The book *Are Prisons Obsolete?* by Angela Davis has greatly helped me to understand why I am incarcerated and how the prison system operates.

Angela Davis seeks to do two things. First, she reveals the impact of prisons on the lives of people on both the inside and the outside. The people punished most harshly are often the inmates' families. Second, she seeks to challenge the "taken for grantedness" of prisons as a necessary and inevitable part of our social system in the United States. She describes the historical development of the prison-industrial complex.

The purpose of prisons, she suggests, has changed over the years. Brutal forms of torture and personal punishment such as whippings, mutilation, and stockades were challenged as inhumane. The Quakers began a movement to provide space for people to repent and to start new lives. If they were penitent, they could move on. Penitentiaries had small cells, like monasteries. But penitence did not work for most. There were broader concerns for rehabilitating and returning people to society healed. Educational intervention and religious conversion were part of prison operations. Because funds were insufficient, offerings for rehabilitation were marginal. Punishment through incarceration then became a central goal. Long sentences have led some to realize that the goal is simply incarceration, the removal of people from society.

I am incarcerated, pulled out of my life for six months, as a form of punishment. My incarceration was not aimed at correcting me or helping me to grow. Work is so minimal it is absurd. Each day, I work about one hour and I wait around for three or four hours to be counted.

Several years ago, John Egerton, a Nashville author, wrote a fine book titled *Speak Now Against the Day*.[7] In the book he examined the civil rights movement prior to 1954 and discovered that civil rights activists did not challenge the separate-but-equal system but sought to make it more humane. They tried to secure equal educational opportunities in the separate school systems. The same applied to equal housing and transportation. Egerton says that few spoke against the separate-but-equal laws. Almost universally, activists tried to negotiate within the system. (It is interesting to note that at first even Martin Luther King Jr. and the Montgomery Association wanted to negotiate within the system.) *Brown v. the Board of Education* showed that the separate-but-equal system and structure were unconstitutional and wrong. They had to be dismantled. With *Brown v. the Board of Education*, a new day had begun. The whole system had to be transformed. We still seek the reality of this transformation.

Davis argues along a similar line. We have tried reforming the prison system, and it has not worked. Racism, sexism, and homophobia are deeply ingrained in the system. The prison system cannot be fixed. It is obsolete. Prisons, as a way to deal with people who commit crimes, are obsolete.

The problem has been compounded by the fact that prisons are a profitable business. There are nine million people in prison throughout the world. Two million of these are in the United States in prisons, jails, youth facilities, and immigrant detention centers. The U.S. claims 5 percent of the world's population, but more than 20 percent of the world's combined prison population. In the late 1960s, there were approximately 200,000 individuals in prison. Now we have ten times that number locked up.

"Are we willing," Davis asks, "to relegate ever larger numbers of people from racially oppressed communities to an isolated existence marked by authoritarian regimes, violence, disease, and technologies of seclusion that produce severe mental instability?"[8]

Why has this happened?

During the Reagan administration, there was a movement to be tough on crime. It was exaggerated in many ways. From this period came legislation leading to certain imprisonment and longer sentences. Power to exercise discretion was taken away from the judges. There was also extensive unemployment and homelessness. Black people were targeted. According to a study conducted in 1995, one in three black men between the ages of twenty and twenty-nine is under the control of the prison system; black women also have been incarcerated at increasingly high numbers.[9]

Segregation ruled the South until a century after the abolition of slavery. The system of exploitation saw black people as property. Such views continue even now. In prisons, racism runs deep. After abolition, blacks were treated as second-class citizens with curtailed voting rights, educational opportunities, and marginal jobs. Lynching was an extralegal institution in which ruthless groups took thousands of lives. We rarely acknowledge the role of race in prisons. Is racism so deeply entrenched in the institution of prisons that it is almost impossible to eliminate? In the prison in Manchester, there are few black staff and officers, although approximately 40 percent of the inmates are black.

After slavery, black codes were established in slave states. Slavery and involuntary servitude had been abolished by the Thirteenth Amendment, but not as punishment for crime. The black codes defined crime, and only black people were convicted. Following slavery, the southern system hastened to establish new restrictions. Vagrancy became a crime punishable by incarceration or forced labor, and convict-leasing programs were prominent.

Being in prison has made me aware of the close relationship of prisons and corporations. The tough-on-crime legislation, which includes long sentences, has led to mass incarceration. More prisons are built every year.

Why is there no major debate on the enormous increase in incarceration? Why is there no discussion about alternatives to prison? Let us begin the debate.

[8]
OCTOBER-NOVEMBER: LOOKING BACK, LOOKING FORWARD

For what has been—thanks!
For what shall be—yes!

—DAG HAMMARSKJÖLD

Friday, October 1, 2004

I am going home. I will see Judy. Both are on my mind, but I am not brooding. I feel at peace, grateful for having survived and for using the time well. I related to the people in prison; dealt with difficulties; enjoyed some things; cursed in my mind at the guard; wrote many letters; spent time in solitude; walked; did other exercise; expressed my thoughts and ideas; and read theology, novels, newspapers, magazines.

At 7:45 a.m. fellow inmates James, Ed, and Robert carried my boxes to the front of the prison. I waited to be processed. At 8:20 Shorty took me over to the main prison complex. I saw Erik as we drove to the parking lot. (What a gift he has been!) I gave the receptionist my papers, and she told me to wait.

Philip and Judy came in. I was fingerprinted again and asked a number of questions. I received the money still in my commissary account and was given final instructions. Then I left. Surprisingly, no one looked in my boxes.

When I got to the parking lot, I danced. I embraced Judy, Philip, and Erik. We went to the Huddle House, since the Mennonite bakery was closed. We

said a prayer and enjoyed a fine conversation as we ate the meal. We arrived home at 2:30 p.m. Yellow bows hung on the door and around the tree in the yard. I was irritated initially because I thought the electric company was going to cut down my trees. Then I realized that the bows were made from the strips of yellow plastic used to keep people from crossing a police line. It was Lauren's way of welcoming me home.

We had just walked into the house when my daughter Rebecca and her children, Rachel and Dylan, appeared. She had decorated the house for me. What a joy it was to see her!

At a welcome gathering held at the Nashville Peace and Justice Center, I spoke with several local television and newspaper reporters. About seventy people attended the event. Bill Ives greeted me with a picture titled "Free Bird" that showed me looking out of a birdhouse.

I read this statement to those who gathered to welcome me home.

I was released from the federal prison in Manchester, Kentucky, on October 1, 2004, at about 8:30 in the morning. Several people were on hand to welcome me.

I thank you who have come to welcome me back and who have supported me through visits, cards, letters, books, and articles while I was in prison. Your support was dazzling! We share a strong bond born of our commitment to justice, peace, and love. Your visits were joyous times and beacons of encouragement.

I am also grateful to the people at SOA Watch, who were always there, connecting me with twenty-six others who also participated in civil disobedience at Fort Benning in November 2003. It was a delight to know that Roy Bourgeois was here to give his witness just a few days ago.

I have learned about prison, prison life, and the prison-industrial complex. I have learned how crime became a winning political slogan. While actual criminal behavior is decreasing, fear engendered by political candidates is used to win elections. Politics built our current prison system with a population larger than that of every other nation in the world. I also learned how prisons are used to avoid dealing with the causes of crime or the issues of health care, living wages, job development and training, and low-cost rental housing. Systematic injustice flowers while military power becomes an idolatry, the major tool used by the  United States to dominate other countries, all under the guise of democracy and a fight against terrorism.

I want to thank the inmates at Manchester Prison who helped me to survive the complexities of the prison system: stand-up counts, sit-down counts, 3:00 a.m. counts, special counts. These men helped me to understand the rules often enforced at whim and wielded as an abuse of power. They made life tolerable. I am grateful to the inmates for their counsel, often every day, when I was hassled or misunderstood. I want also to thank several guards who showed respect to me and to others. They earned my respect and recognition of their authority. Often, though, there were only the rules, enforced without consistency, continuity, or any effort at interpretation.

I have been empowered by the memory of people—simple, courageous people—throughout Latin America, who faced violence and brutality at the hands of military forces trained in aggressive and abusive military procedures. Graduates of SOA/WHINSEC continue their work in one Latin American country after another. The military preserve the elite and serve the corporate interests of the United States by maintaining stability in Latin America. These corporations pay little tax to help build up the nation while they pay low wages, undermine the people's efforts to exert influence, destroy the possibility for decent health care, and harm the environment. Death squads augment the military. On September 7, three union leaders were assassinated. The president of Colombia has blessed the death squads as they seek to maintain the nation's economic inequalities. Contempt for the rule of law has become widespread in Latin America and in our government.

Long ago, God heard the cry of the people of Israel, who were enslaved and brutally treated. I am grateful for people who speak up so that the cry of people suffering throughout the world will be heard. I am grateful for those who speak amidst the noise of our culture and the deceptions that characterize public life and politics.

We, the people, must find ways to speak truth. We can respond to the cries of the oppressed by securing passage of House Bill 1258, which seeks to close SOA/WHINSEC until a serious investigation into the activities of its graduates is completed. We can also secure passage of legislation to bring justice to our unjust correctional system.

I am glad to be back in Nashville with all of you. Thank you.

—⚬—

After the official welcome, Judy and I ate a delicious meal together. It was good to relax with her.

Saturday, October 2

I am sitting in my reading chair in my study at home. I slept well last night. This morning a raccoon was outside my window getting food from the bird feeders.

Sunday, October 3

My morning pattern is not yet clear to me. Arising at 4:00 a.m. may still be best.

At the early worship service at Edgehill United Methodist Church, the congregation welcomed me, and I felt the depth of their care and concern.

Over breakfast, Judy and I read a fine article about me by Dwight Lewis of the *Tennessean*.[1] What an honor to be recognized in such a way! I am humbled.

O God, you have guided me to this place in my life. It has been a long journey with many times of anxiety and confusion. The decision to cross the line was momentous for me and for others too. Thank you for your blessings.

Judy and I attended the 11:00 a.m. service at Hillsboro Presbyterian Church, where I was recognized by the minister and the congregation.

I prepared for the 3:00 p.m. event at which I would talk about my six months in prison. The chapel at Downtown Presbyterian Church was filled with friends and others who attended as a witness to God's love and justice.

We left the event early because we will leave early tomorrow for Atlanta to see Ed and Murphy, our friends at the Open Door Community.

Bless the day.

WELCOME BACK TO A MAN OF GOD WHO PAID A HIGH PRICE
by Dwight Lewis

Nashville's Downtown Presbyterian Church should be overflowing this afternoon when a liturgy of celebration is held for Don Beisswenger and friends.

Beisswenger returned home to Nashville Friday after spending a six-month federal prison term at the Federal Correctional Institution in Manchester, Ky., on a trespassing conviction. The sentence stemmed from a November 2003 conviction after he pleaded guilty to protesting outside a military base at Fort Benning, Ga., earlier that month.

"The celebration is an opportunity for us to welcome back and honor Don for his witness to peace and justice," said Kathy Masulis, a personal friend and board president of the Penuel Ridge Retreat Center in Cheatham County, which Beisswenger helped found in 1984.

"We live in such a tumultuous time that it's easy to become almost paralyzed with fear and indecisiveness. But Don has shown us that it is possible to take a stand to put our faith into action and to make a personal sacrifice in order to live out our beliefs.

"Not all of us are called to do prison time, but we who profess belief in a God of love are called to witness on behalf of the poor."

When Beisswenger, a retired Vanderbilt University Divinity School professor and a Nashville minister, entered his guilty plea, he stood before U.S. District Judge G. Mallon Faircloth and said:

"I stand before you, a 73-year-old man who is guilty but proud to be able to make this witness."

He was one of more than two dozen activists arrested Nov. 28, 2003 as more than 1,000 people protested in an act of civil disobedience toward the U.S. government's operation of a military school for Latin American soldiers.

The school, which was once called the School of the Americas, is now known as the Western Hemisphere Institute for Security Cooperation.

In an interview last January before being ordered to start serving his prison sentence, Beisswenger told me over the telephone that he considers the military school "a training school on our land."

"That's the type of thing (Osama) bin Laden did," he said. "They're being trained in the method of learning how to execute, kidnap."

While he was incarcerated, Beisswenger stayed in touch with friends mainly through letters.

"I have been thinking about you these days as well as the people of Latin

America," he said in one letter he wrote to friends. "It is raining here at the prison, a dreary day. Yet, I feel alive and my spirits are good, mainly because of the community of persons with whom I share this life, this journey." . . .

Beisswenger later wrote that "I receive courage from knowing that God is the only one before whom we bow down and that God's purposes are sure and not to be confused with our apprehension of them." . . .

Don Beisswenger is indeed a courageous man. His participation in the protest at the military base in Fort Benning, Ga., in November 2003 was the second time he had committed such an act.

He said he did it because "I am a post-Holocaust Christian who learned that Christian nations can too easily ignore brutality and atrocities done in their name.

"We must always seek to obey God rather than humans. My faith has also led me to be attentive to what I call a war against the poor. The shaping of policies which enrich the few and dishonor the poor, especially children, has become the tragedy of our time."

How lucky Middle Tennessee and this nation are to have heroes such as Don Beisswenger. And it's great to have him back home. Let's turn out this afternoon at the Downtown Presbyterian Church at 154 Fifth Ave. N., to let him know how much we appreciate him and what he's done to make this world a better place to live.

Dwight Lewis is a columnist, regional editor, and member of the editorial board for *The Tennessean*.

Saturday, November 13

A letter to family and friends

This will be my last letter specifically related to my life in prison. Of course, the experience has set in motion much thought, prayer, and reflection; and I will be thinking about its meanings for a long time. But now I will move into postprison life deliberately and with a hope for clarity in the ways I live. Life seems like a fugue. Various themes intertwine to make the melody, but the melody is not always evident. The themes are there, but the whole has not come together. Eventually I will hear the melody. I trust that to happen.

Judy and me at The Open Door in Atlanta
a few days after my release

In some ways, I have been clear about my life after prison. I will continue my efforts to protest the war against the poor. I will be involved with the Living Room and with the homeless coalition; and I will continue my work for low-income housing. My concern about the world's poor and oppressed people will find expression in efforts to close SOA/WHINSEC.

However, my life after prison is problematic. The structure of my former life, through which I engaged the world, no longer seems to work. I seem confused and a bit uninterested. Former themes are less clear. Issues related to prisons and criminal justice have emerged as a concern. I left five hundred men in prison, most of whom should be home with their families and at work. So I am taking more time to let what is happening in and around me percolate and speak. God is in the midst of it all.

My release from prison was routine. I was told what I could take with me. Everything that was given to me in prison will stay in prison. I did take a bright orange knit hat, though, because it reminded me of my first day in prison.

I was released on October 1 at 9:00 a.m. Judy Pilgrim, Philip Beisswenger, and Erik Johnson met me.

We arrived in Nashville about 2:00 p.m. After a brief time at home, we went to the welcoming at the Peace and Justice Center, a joyous affair for me. What a joy to see all the people in my life! On Sunday, at a time of worship, prayer, and reflection at Downtown Presbyterian Church, I expressed my initial observations of what had occurred. It was a moving event and a time to discern where God had been present in the midst of it all.

The injustice perpetuated by graduates of SOA/WHINSEC persists. Solid records report their actions, especially in Colombia, where recently three union leaders were killed by the military, most of whom were trained at SOA/WHINSEC. House Bill 1258, with 138 sponsors, still needs to the passed by the House. It would close the school until a serious, externally controlled investigation can be conducted.

How do I live in this world now? What will be the focus of my attention in the next months? I received a letter from Gary, one of the SOA 27 with whom I was arrested. He quoted Liz McAlister: "Don't get weary in the face of a world that has embraced endless war and bankrupting military spending ($12,000 every second of every day), a world where lies pass for truth, sound bites for wisdom, arrogance for understanding."[2] Like many of you, I take her assessment seriously for my life.

Where is the source of our hope? What keeps us from getting weary? Jesus promised truth, light, and peace, not a palliative peace but a peace that goes deeper and challenges us. Don't get weary, he says, for I am with you. Christ's promise of peace remains a ground of hope for me.

So I journey on. We journey together, honoring the creation and seeking to bear witness to God's love and justice.

With love and affection,

Don

Monday, November 15

A letter to inmates at Manchester Prison

It has been six weeks since I was released from Manchester Prison. I have been resting, but also trying to gain some clarity about what being in prison has done to me—and to you. I am grateful for the way you all befriended me, taught me, and kept me out of the solitary housing unit!

I was greeted with a homecoming when I got back that Friday afternoon, October 1. I was glad because I wanted many people to know about SOA/WHINSEC. The terrorism, kidnapping, and torture done by its graduates are done in our country's name and with our taxes. We must try to close the school if we can. My time in prison helped me in my attempts to let the truth about the SOA/WHINSEC be known.

I have spoken here and there, not only about SOA/WHINSEC, but also about my prison experience. I studied the criminal justice system by personal experience as well as by reading about it. In my speaking, I tell about the inequities in sentencing as well as the problem of using conspiracy as a charge on which to base arrests. I say that most everyone at the prison is not violent and could be home working and caring for loved ones.

I was interviewed on the radio and television yesterday. I spoke of how we use prisons to avoid dealing with the lack of jobs that provide a living wage, the lack of affordable health care, and the limited resources for adequate education. I have spoken several times at large gatherings.

Thank you for helping me understand all this as well as helping me survive. I count you as friends. Friends are special people who become a part of your life for no particular reason except to meet together and to enjoy life as much as they can. Friends help us to care about ourselves and others. They help us consider our confusion, our anxiety, and the deeper feelings under the surface. Sometimes they encourage us to think about justice, love, and peace, not only for ourselves, but for all people.

I remember each of you with joy:

> Jayber told me again and again to stand straight and to take bigger strides.
> Will taught me by being such a fine coach and courteous person.
> Saxter helped me to stay out of trouble, to laugh, and to play spades a bit better.
> Don helped keep me politically informed.
> Simon reached out to me and made me a desk from a cardboard box.
> Jay made me feel comfortable using the laundry room for reading.
> Dick, my bunkie, informed me of the many things I should and should not do. He helped me survive while we lived between the microwave and telephone for those five weeks.
> Darby and Stack helped with birthday gifts.
> Brent was a consultant and a considerate guide along the way.
> Johnny was a friendly presence with a great smile.
> Mick helped me relate to people in the religious community.
> Curtis kept me laughing, even if he was a bit ornery at times.
> Eb answered my questions.
> Larry kept me alert by routinely asking, "How's it going, Mr. B?"
> Charles helped me relate to people I wanted to understand better.
> Reid and I enjoyed playing cribbage.
> Patrick helped me understand the places where I was vulnerable.
> Several of you helped me exercise.

John and I shared our concerns about diabetes.
Red bantered with me on occasion.
Doral was another person like me, a bit older, whose company I enjoyed.
Doo and I had several fine conversations.
Hill left, but I appreciated his courtesy.
Monroe was a joy, even though he kidded me a lot.
Ned and Tony engaged me in thinking about the Bible as a guide.
James and I talked on occasion, and he helped me carry my stuff out.
Jerry and I argued about biblical authority—conversations I found helpful.
I also had arguments with the guards, chaplains, and staff, but I found they
    were at times courteous and kind.

These are some of the things I appreciate about you:

Some of you showed care and concern for your partners and your children.
Some of you spoke with bitterness and anger, but then your love surfaced; and
    I was glad.
Separation from families was difficult, and you coped with it the best you could.
Many of you lost important jobs while in prison and knew that getting work
    again would be difficult. I hope you find a way to use your gifts creatively.
You were generous in sharing food. I was amazed by how many of you cooked
    meals.

As you know, I am concerned about social justice. I believe in justice in our nation's foreign policies and fairness in the criminal justice system. Several of you have worked on your own cases, but you were also concerned about the criminal justice system and specifically about sentence reform.

I learned how crime is used in political campaigns and why elected legislators call for more prisons. In 1980, about 300,000 people were in prison. Now, some twenty-five years later, two million people are in prison. Why? During this time, the crime rate was going down. The drug laws were central to the increase in the prison population, as was the profitability of prisons for businesses. Now we have so many people in prison that our prison population is higher than any other country in the world.

I send my best wishes and hopes that you will find life despite the boundaries, the counts, and the abuse of power that you experience.

Don Beisswenger

—⁂—

An essay written by my granddaughter Sara Beisswenger, age nine

"I'm going to jail," my grandfather said on the walk we were on together.

Those words took me by surprise. My grandfather wasn't a bad man, was he? At first I didn't know what to say; then questions popped into my head. "How?" I asked. "Why?"

My dad had gone down to Columbus, Georgia, to see my grandfather, who lived in Tennessee. I asked him about it when he got home, but I didn't get any answers. I didn't know what had happened, but I was going to find out.

It ended up that my grandfather wanted to tell me himself, so he came to my house for the weekend. When we went on a walk around my neighborhood, he talked about God's plan for him, and then he just said it. He told me he was going to be in jail for six months in Kentucky. Then he told me why. While he talked, I stayed quiet. I didn't know what to say.

He started out telling me how much he loved me. Then he said that every year, down in Georgia, he protests at a camp that trains South American men to be army men. He told me how nineteen men who had graduated from this camp had gone into a small town in South America and killed everyone in the town. Only one woman survived. He thought that was terrible and wanted to stop it from happening again. I agreed.

Then he told me that people can protest all they want, but if there is violence or if they walk on private property, they can get arrested. He said that he took six steps onto the army base where the camp is located, and he kneeled in prayer. He was arrested along with twenty-six other people who did the same thing. He was not sorry for what he had done.

I am very happy that he is out now. He probably could have walked out, but then he would have had to stay in jail longer. There was a baseball field the prisoners could go to. It wasn't a bad place. But I feel for my dad. It's not easy having your father in jail.

Now I think about God and God's plan for me. I look up to my grandfather for doing what he did. I think he did a very good thing.

AFTERWORD

My six months in a federal prison have made me see life differently. They have shaped me and in some ways become a definitive time in my life. In the preface, I indicated three themes—my interior, interpersonal, and public life—each a dimension of human life that provided a perspective from which to understand my experience in prison. I conclude by saying a brief word about each and a bit about their meaning within the context of God's presence in the world.

My interior life was stretched as I coped with my new social reality. I felt vulnerable, tired, hopeful, thankful, joyful, cautious, fearful. I missed being touched by others and the freedom to come and go as I pleased. I survived by finding moments of solitude and by paying attention to my interior life.

I understood the psalmist's cry, "You, O LORD, are my hope" (Ps. 71:5). God was present for me while I was incarcerated, and I maintained my relationship with the sacred, the holy, throughout the time. I was able to see events in which God was present and to discover meaning in situations where I did not see it at first. Reverence for God gave me reverence for life. Yet I also knew the absence of God, darkness, and confusion.

I survived and even prospered. Not having my own space in which to live and sleep distorted my first few weeks in prison. Yet I discovered that confinement was also a gift. It was not all struggle, disrespect, and pain. I experienced joy.

Second, a community of people graced my life—family (my siblings, children, and grandchildren), friends, colleagues, inmates, and even officers on occasion. Inmates guided me through the system and helped me avoid serious conflict. Visitors buoyed my spirits each week as we talked, told stories, and broke bread. People wrote notes and letters about their lives and offered me encouragement. Poetry and jokes gave me strength for the day. I found new

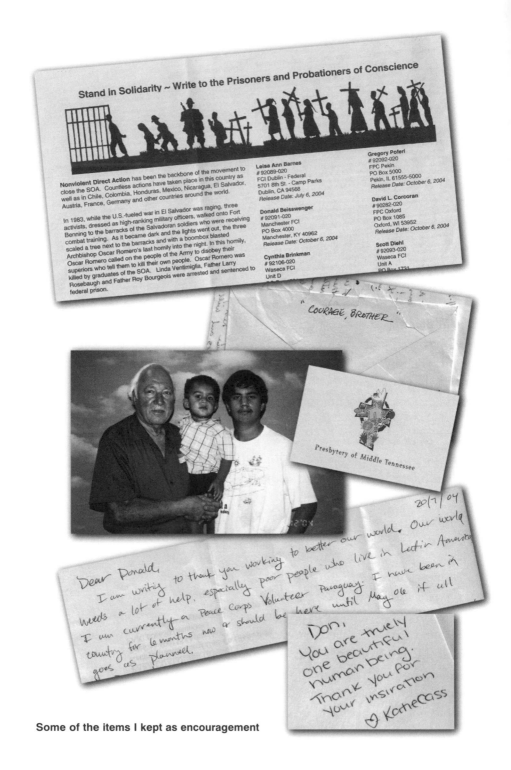

Some of the items I kept as encouragement

meaning in relationships as I corresponded with friends. A communion of saints surrounded me. The faculty of the Vanderbilt University Divinity School offered me support, which I valued deeply.

The Presbyterian Peace Fellowship honored me and other prisoners of conscience with their Peaceseeker Award.

Judy Pilgrim and I learned more about each other from week to week. A prison courtship is difficult. Separation is costly, but we had time almost every week to talk about many things: children, money, conflict, needs for solitude, calls to relate to others. The Holy One was vital to our maturing relationship. I was honored and grateful for this key aspect of my life in community.

Public life was always a vital part of my identity and work. In prison it was severely restricted and always under scrutiny by the authorities. As the only prisoner of conscience at the Manchester prison, I was a puzzle to the other prisoners and the guards, even though I kept a low profile. On several occasions, when people were intimidated, I felt called to act for justice.

I wrote to my congressman and encouraged others to write letters protesting SOA/WHINSEC and calling for an investigation of the school and its graduates. I read about prisons and developed convictions about the criminal justice system, the privatization of prisons, racism within the justice system, overly long sentences for nonviolent crimes, and excessive control and humiliation of inmates.

Public life became most difficult upon my release. The constraints of prison made public action by the inmates impossible. I left with their strong encouragement to tell about the mistreatment that goes on there. At the same time, I was committed to seek the closing of SOA/WHINSEC. I also had an ongoing commitment to work on issues related to poverty and homelessness in Nashville as well as in Latin America and around the world.

Yet as I prepared to be released and to leave the people I had come to know in prison, I experienced a deep melancholy. I lamented the state of our nation, which relies so heavily on military power and violence. Wars consume our resources. The military, corporations, and politics converge to dominate the nation and the world. We create more potent weapons to secure our power while making empty promises to the poor and showing contempt for those who suffer. We abuse God's wondrous creation, which is now part of the world's poverty. The workings of our nation are oiled by the blood of those disregarded by the onslaught of industrialization and corporate interest.

Thirty years ago, I spent a month in Colombia learning about injustice, conflict, and violence in that battered country. I also visited Christian communities alive with concern for justice. I was involved in a program organized by Mennonites and Catholics and aimed at helping North Americans understand Latin American life, politics, culture, and religion. The program focused on how the message of God in Jesus brings good news to the poor as it forms community. I was converted to new, deeper understandings of the gospel as seen through the eyes of the poor. Key to my new perspective was being present with the poor, oppressed, marginalized, and imprisoned and learning to think and act from their point of view. This has been a key feature of my life since I returned to the United States. It has shaped my work in theological education, my life in the church, and my life as a citizen.

Philip Berrigan once said, "The poor tell us who we are. The prophets tell us who we could be. So we hide the poor and kill the prophets."

Thus it has been and continues to be. Since my conversion to the poor, my life has changed. Proximity to the poor has become a definitive part of my life. My energies have been directed toward the margins of society. There my faith in the God of Jesus Christ was given form.

I am now seventy-seven years of age and bringing to a conclusion some parts of my life, but I continue on in hope.

In Testimony: The Word Made Fresh, Daniel Berrigan says, "We live with a sense that the best efforts we put out change very little of a vast apparatus of destruction and despair. The times are like a hand that closes on our throat."[1] But the power of God works to keep alive the reality of love, justice, hope, and kindness. Alleluia!

APPENDIX A
THE SCHOOL OF THE AMERICAS

The School of the Americas (SOA) opened in Panama in 1946. After a critical investigation in 2001 by Congress and the United Nations, it was renamed Western Hemisphere Institute for Security and Cooperation (WHINSEC). With a new name, it was hoped that SOA could distance itself from past atrocities, avoid responsibility for the behavior of its graduates throughout Latin America, and moderate strong opposition by the School of the Americas Watch.

Throughout its history, the school has trained more than 60,000 Latin American police and military officers in the tactics of counterinsurgency. Alumni of the school include some of the most brutal military dictators and human-rights violators in Latin America. Officers trained at the school carry out the mission of the United States Southern Command, protecting the interests of the United States in Latin America. Organizers, religious leaders, teachers, students, health care workers, and other human rights activists are considered security threats.

The SOA was expelled from Panama in 1984 under the terms of the Panama Canal Treaties. It reopened the same year at Fort Benning, Georgia, where it continues to offer training in the techniques of counterinsurgency. People in Latin America refer to the school as *La Escuela de Asesinos*, the School of Assassins, because of its documented legacy of torture, execution, massacre, displacement, and forced disappearance of thousands of noncombatants in Latin America.

Two of the three military officers responsible for the 1980 assassination of San Salvador's Archbishop Oscar Romero; three of the five officers involved in the 1980 rapes and murders of four churchwomen from the United States;

and ten of the twelve cited for the 1981 massacre of more than 750 women, children, and men in the village of El Mozote were graduates of the SOA. The United Nations Truth Commission cited nineteen graduates among the twenty-six officers responsible for the 1989 assassination of six Jesuit priests, along with a mother and daughter. One hundred of the 246 soldiers cited for continuing atrocities in Colombia are also graduates. The Guatemalan military intelligence agency played a central role in the 1998 assassination of human rights champion Bishop Juan Gerardi. In February 2005, a Colombian paramilitary squad brutally murdered three union workers. The eleventh brigade of the Colombian army, trained at the SOA, assassinated Luis Eduardo Guerra, a human rights leader, along with three children.

Of the many hundreds of graduates implicated in the atrocities and war crimes, only a few have faced prosecution. Some have returned to be instructors at the school. Others have been invited back to speak and are included in the SOA/WHINSEC Hall of Fame.

Opponents of the school have gathered annually since 1990 in the largest nonviolent direct-action campaign in United States history, yet the movement is generally disregarded by the news media. Persistence and courage have been the strength of the movement against SOA/WHINSEC. Every November, college students, women, members of monastic groups, clergy, labor leaders, war veterans, older adults, youth, congressional leaders, and actors converge at the entrance to Fort Benning, Georgia, for a vigil. The 2005 weekend vigil brought together more than 19,000 people. The heart of the vigil is the reading of the names of men, women, and children who have disappeared or been killed by graduates of the school. As each name is read, the gathering responds, *"Presente!"* (Present).

The SOA Watch began in 1990 after the 1989 assassination of six priests, their coworker, and her teenage daughter in El Salvador. Rev. Roy Bourgeois, a former missionary to Bolivia who knew the priests, rented an apartment at the entrance to the SOA and with several friends held the first vigil and protest. Through public speaking, fasting, research, and creative acts of nonviolent resistance that sometimes led to imprisonment, the SOA Watch has given witness to the sordid history of the School of the Americas. Atrocities continue in Latin America and elsewhere, especially in Colombia, Guantánamo Bay, Iraq, and secret prisons of torture.

Military dishonesty and duplicity will continue, as will protest and non-violent resistance. The goal of SOA Watch is to close the school until a serious investigation is completed, the atrocities are documented, and the people responsible are punished. The larger goal of the SOA Watch focuses on changing military policies and practices around the world.

APPENDIX B

My statement to Judge Faircloth, January 26, 2004

Your Honor, thank you for this opportunity to address the court.

I stand before you to state my plea.

I carefully considered my actions on November 23. They were made possible, in part, by the death of my wife of forty-nine years, which gave me freedom to act. They also resulted from my study and research, over the last twenty-three years, into the political and economic dynamics of Latin America. I started my study in earnest when I heard of the rape and murder of four missionaries in El Salvador. They, along with Archbishop Romero, had challenged the seventeen families who owned most of the land in El Salvador and who resented any idea of land reform. To protect their land, the families' security forces became death squads. Upon further exploration, I found that the death squads were related to the military and that the worst human-rights abuses were executed by graduates of the School of the Americas.

I began to protest in various ways, which finally led to my crossing the line in 1999 and going around a concrete abutment last November.

I am a Presbyterian minister and a professor emeritus at Vanderbilt University School of Divinity. However, I am also a post-Holocaust Christian who learned that Christian nations too easily ignore brutality and atrocities done in their name. We must always seek to obey God rather than human beings. My faith has led me to be attentive to what I call the war against the poor. The shaping of policies that enrich the few and dishonor the poor, especially children, has become the tragedy of our time. The poor are losers in the counterinsurgency warfare that is carried out by the military forces in Latin America. Those who seek change, speak up, or organize against violent acts of the military become enemies and often victims.

The SOA/WHINSEC must own up to its complicity in the crimes of its graduates. Amnesty International has said, "The U.S. government should take immediate steps to establish an independent commission to investigate the past activities of the SOA and its graduates and to recommend appropriate reparations for any violations of humans rights to which training at the SOA contributed, including criminal prosecution, redress for victims and their families, and a public apology." If the school were held accountable, I could more easily, in the tradition of Martin Luther King Jr. and Mahatma Gandhi, state my guilt. But we do not look carefully at what SOA graduates have done in our name, nor have we acknowledged our complicity in their acts of terrorism.

Yet I do honor the rule of law, which is so easily transgressed by those in power. I honor the law even with its many injustices. Thus I plead guilty, but reluctantly. I acknowledge that I trespassed onto the base at Ft. Benning, Georgia, on November 23, 2003, at about 2:30 p.m. I also recognize that I did not abide by the ban-and-bar letter I was given in 1999; I acted last November without even thinking about the letter.

This decision has been difficult, since it is the SOA/WHINSEC that has violated the norms of our nation in training the military leaders of Latin American countries, leaders who have been involved in so many atrocities. In my judgment and in the judgment of many others, the School of the Americas is guilty. Its guilt is for crimes far greater than my six steps around that concrete abutment.

I stand before you, a seventy-three-year-old man who is guilty but proud to be able to make this witness.

APPENDIX C

DIVINITY SCHOOL

The faculty of the Divinity School of Vanderbilt University stands with and declares its support for our friend and former colleague, Don Beisswenger. Don has recently been sentenced to six months in a federal prison and fined $1,000 for his act of civil disobedience in protesting the work of the Western Hemisphere Institute for Security Cooperation, formerly known as the School of the Americas.

At Fort Benning, Georgia, the base that houses WHISC, Don and more than twenty others joined a much larger group that had previously done the same.

Taking a few steps into Fort Benning, they attempted to call the nation's attention to the program that has, for more than two decades, produced graduates who have committed human rights atrocities in several Latin American countries.

We commit ourselves and urge others to learn more about the United States' foreign policy in Latin America and to seek a Congressional investigation of the work of WHISC.

We, the undersigned members of the Divinity School faculty, express our admiration for Don Beisswenger's enduring witness on this issue of human rights in our hemisphere. We further declare that his chosen path for that witness is consistent with the best traditions and commitments of the Vanderbilt Divinity School.

James Hudnut-Beumler
Daniel Patte
Alice W. Hunt
Robin M. Jensen
Victor Anderson
J. Patout Burns
Viki Matson
Mark Justad
Kathelen Flake
James P. Byrd
Jay Geller

Bonnie Miller-McLemore
Jack Sasson
Mark Miller-McLemore
Leonard Hummel
John Thatamanil
John McClure
Amy-Jill Levine
Annalisa Azzoni
Trudy H. Stringer
Joanne Sandberg
C. Melissa Snarr
Bill Hook

Paul DeHart
Dale Johnson
David Buttrick
Forrest E. Harris, Sr.
Lloyd Lewis
L. Susan Bond
Edward Farley
Walter Harrelson
J. Jackson Forstman
Eugene TeSelle
Frank Gulley
Victor Judge

QUESTIONS FOR FURTHER REFLECTION

On the interior dimensions of life

1. What role did vulnerability and survival play in Don's incarceration?
2. How did they lead to stress, confusion, languishing? What was vital for Don's recovery and healing?
3. In what ways are vulnerability and survival significant in your life? How are they expressed in your feelings? thoughts? actions?
4. In what ways does Don struggle to understand his calling? Why was it important to have sacred work to do?
5. The author states that there is a geography to faith; our calling changes depending on where we are. What is your calling? What sacred work do you do?
6. How did Don discover and acknowledge holy presence? What were the results of his personal relationship with God?
7. How were solitude and prayer vital to Don?
8. In what ways was confinement a gift for Don?

On interpersonal dimensions of life

1. Consider Don's efforts to become friends with fellow inmates. What were some of his frustrations? Recall any experiences you've had when you reached out but had difficulty making a connection. How did you proceed in those situations?
2. How did Don relate to the guards and staff? What was the importance of rules? of clearly defined relationships between staff and prisoners?
3. How would you describe Don's relationship with his visitors? family? friends? How do difficult and supportive relationships balance in your life?

4. Why did people come to visit Don in prison? In what ways did they give him hope?
5. Sixty percent of prison inmates have no visitors and receive no mail. How do you respond to the gospel's call to visit prisoners after reading this account of one man's time in prison?
6. The author had a special relationship with Judy Pilgrim. What difference did it make to him in prison?
7. What role did faith communities play in Don's life before his incarceration? during his time in prison? after his release?
8. What role does the community of faith play in your life?

On public dimensions of life

1. What did you notice about the role of public religion in the lives of the inmates? the author? How did you feel about the chaplains' interaction with Don and other inmates?
2. Support of the author translated into support for closing the School of the Americas for some people. How do your personal and public loyalties intertwine?
3. Think about the role of prisons. How would you describe their function? How does Don's experience and the information he shares affect your understanding of the prison system?
4. How did Don express his concern for issues of war and peace, militarism and nonviolence? How do you express your faith in relationship to issues of public concern?
5. How do you feel called to become more involved in public concerns, such as issues related to war and peace? the prison system?

On the dynamics among the interior, interpersonal, and public dimensions of human life— especially of Christian existence grounded in wholeness and integrity

1. How did Don's interior life affect his public life? How did his public life affect his interior life?
2. In what aspects of life was Don free? What is the nature of freedom in your own life?

3. How did the author's concern for closing the School of the Americas intersect with his interpersonal life? his interior life? How do the interior, interpersonal, and public dimensions of your life intersect?
4. In which aspects of your life do you experience the presence of God?

NOTES

CHAPTER 1: FROM PROTEST TO PRISON

Epigraph. Leonardo Boff, *Passion of Christ, Passion of the World: The Facts, Their Interpretation, and Their Meaning Yesterday and Today*, trans. Robert R. Barr (Maryknoll, NY: Orbis Books, 1987), 124.

1. Dietrich Bonhoeffer, *Life Together*, trans. John W. Doberstein (New York: Harper & Brothers, 1954), 77.

2. J. William Fulbright, *The Arrogance of Power* (New York: Random House, 1967).

CHAPTER 2: APRIL: ENTERING THE PRISON SYSTEM

Epigraph. Jerome G. Miller, "American Gulag," *YES!: A Journal of Positive Futures*, no. 15 (Fall 2000): 16. Available at
http://www.yesmagazine.org/article.asp?ID=371

1. Matt Pulle, "An Old Man Behind Bars," *Nashville Scene* (March 4–10, 2004). Available at http://www.nashvillescene.com/Stories/News/2004/03/04/An_Old_Man_Behind_Bars/index.shtml.

2. Frances Willard, quoted in *The Beacon Book of Quotations by Women*, comp. Rosalie Maggio (Boston: Beacon Press, 1992), 62.

CHAPTER 3: MAY: SETTLING IN

Epigraph. Azar Nafisi, *Reading Lolita in Tehran: A Memoir in Books* (New York: Random House, 2004), 326.

1. Original drawing by Don Peterson. Used by permission.

2. Dietrich Bonhoeffer, *Letters and Papers from Prison*, ed. Eberhard Bethge (New York: Touchstone, 1997).

3. Rainer Maria Rilke, *Letters to a Young Poet*, trans. M. D. Herter Norton (New York: W. W. Norton, 1934), 64.

4. David J. Garrow, *Bearing the Cross: Martin Luther King, Jr., and the Southern Christian Leadership Conference* (New York: HarperCollins Publishers, 2004).

CHAPTER 4: JUNE: SURVIVING

Epigraph. Penny Lernoux, quoted in Robert Ellsberg, *All Saints: Daily Reflections on Saints, Prophets, and Witnesses for Our Time* (New York: Crossroad Publishing Company, 1997), 439–40.

1. Karen Armstrong, *The Spiral Staircase: My Climb out of Darkness* (New York: Alfred A. Knopf, 2004).

2. Ibid., 35.

3. Ibid., 28.

4. Bonhoeffer, *Letters and Papers from Prison*, 8.

5. Ibid., 176–77.

6. Vassar Miller, "Without Ceremony," in *If I Had Wheels or Love: Collected Poems of Vassar Miller* (Dallas: Southern Methodist University Press, 1991), 35.

CHAPTER 5: JULY: BEING CONFINED

1. Robert McCammon, *Boy's Life* (New York: Pocket Books, 1992), 206.

2. William O. Douglas, quoted in Nat Hentoff, *The War on the Bill of Rights—and the Gathering Resistance* (New York: Seven Stories Press, 2003), 158.

3. Desmond Tutu, *God Has a Dream: A Vision of Hope for Our Time* (New York: Doubleday, 2004), 14–15.

4. R. S. Thomas, "The Presence," *Later Poems: A Selection* (London: Macmillan, 1983), 152.

CHAPTER 6: AUGUST: REFLECTING

Epigraph. Henri J. M. Nouwen, *Bread for the Journey: A Daybook of Wisdom and Faith* (San Francisco: HarperSanFrancisco, 1997), January 12.

1. Will D. Campbell, *Robert G. Clark's Journey to the House: A Black Politician's Story* (Jackson, MS: University Press of Mississippi, 2003).

2. Pope Paul VI, quoted in Ellsberg, *All Saints*, 337.

3. Jonathan Schell, "Strong and Wrong," *The Nation* 279, no. 5 (August 16/23, 2004): 7.

4. Eberhard Bethge, *Dietrich Bonhoeffer: A Biography* (Minneapolis: Augsburg Fortress Publishers, 2000).

5. Emily Dickinson, "XLVI," in *The Collected Poems of Emily Dickinson* (New York: Barnes & Noble Classics, 2003), 210–11.

6. Graham Greene, *The Power and the Glory* (New York: Penguin Classics, 2003).

7. Martha Whitmore Hickman, *Healing after Loss: Daily Meditations for Working through Grief* (New York: HarperCollins, 1994).

8. Ibid., July 30. Original quotation is from Dag Hammarskjöld, *Markings*, trans. Leif Sjöberg and W. H. Auden (New York: Alfred A. Knopf, 1964), 174.

9. Flannery O'Connor, quoted in Ellsberg, *All Saints*, 332.

10. Vincent van Gogh, quoted in Ibid., 324.

11. Flannery O'Connor, quoted in Ibid., 331.

12. Sasha Abramsky, *Hard Time Blues: How Politics Built a Prison Nation* (New York: St. Martin's Press/Thomas Dunne Books, 2002).

13. Helen Keller, *Light in My Darkness*, ed. Ray Silverman (West Chester, PA: Swedenborg, 1994), 15.

CHAPTER 7: SEPTEMBER: LEAVING PRISON

Epigraph. Boff, *Passion of Christ, Passion of the World*, 125.

1. William Sloane Coffin, *Credo* (Louisville, KY: Westminster John Knox Press, 2004), 67.

2. Jim Hightower, "Bush Zones Go National," *The Nation* (August 16/23, 2004): 28.

3. Pope Paul VI, quoted in Ellsberg, *All Saints*, 338.

4. Frederick W. Faber, "There's a Wideness in God's Mercy, " *The United Methodist Hymnal* (Nashville: United Methodist Publishing House, 1989), no. 121.

5. Merriam-Webster OnLine, http://www.merriam-webster.com/dictionary/languish.

6. Angela Y. Davis, *Are Prisons Obsolete?* (New York: Seven Stories Press, 2003).

7. John Egerton, *Speak Now Against the Day: The Generation Before the Civil Rights Movement in the South* (Chapel Hill, NC: University of North Carolina Press, 1995).

8. Davis, *Are Prisons Obsolete?*, 10.

9. Ibid., 19.

CHAPTER 8: OCTOBER–NOVEMBER: LOOKING BACK, LOOKING FORWARD

Epigraph. From *The Doubleday Christian Quotation Collection*, comp. Hannah Ward and Jennifer Wild (New York: Doubleday, 1997), 269.

1. Dwight Lewis, "Welcome Back to a Man of God Who Paid a High Price," *The Tennessean* (Oct. 3, 2004): 25A.

2. Elizabeth McAlister, "'Don't Get Weary'—17th Annual May Action at Project ELF," *Nukewatch Quarterly* (Summer 2004): 1. Available online at http://www.nukewatch.com/quarterly/20042summer/20042page1.

AFTERWORD

1. Daniel Berrigan, *Testimony: The Word Made Fresh* (Maryknoll, NY: Orbis Books, 2004), 159.

EXTENSION OF COPYRIGHT PAGE

ABOUT THE AUTHOR

D on Beisswenger holds degrees from Macalester College and Yale Divinity School. He was ordained to ministry in the Presbyterian Church in 1956, the year he married Joyce Horton.

Don and Joyce served congregations in the Ozark Mountains, Cincinnati, and Iowa before they moved to Chicago in 1962 to work on assembly lines and develop a business-industrial ministry. He also traveled to the South to register African American voters. Don says, "I put my shoulder to the plow of overcoming racism and economic injustice." Once, when black friends were prevented from buying a house, he and Joyce bought the house and then resold it to them, despite threats and harassment.

In 1968 Don joined the Vanderbilt Divinity School as a professor and director of field education, guiding students to connect religious faith with personal and social existence. This work brought national recognition to the divinity school for the excellence of the field studies program.

In 1983 Don and Joyce founded the Penuel Ridge Contemplative Retreat Center in Tennessee.

After retiring from Vanderbilt in 1996, Don continued to work on behalf of the poor and homeless in Nashville and to study the oppressed poor in Latin America.

"I can do all things through Christ who strengthens me."

I admire your courage!

Stay Strong

♥ —Sara A.

Dear Don—

I'm proud of you, but so sorry for your troubles. Even for a good cause, prison can't be much fun. If you let me know (even through my folks!) your address I'll write while you're locked up & look forward to the time this is behind instead of before you—

Under the mercy,

Ward

When through the deep waters I call thee to go,

The rivers of woe shall not thee overflow;

For I will be with thee, thy troubles to bless,

And sanctify to thee, thy deepest distress.

Dear popey

I am getting a pet lizerd it is called the leppert gecko. I am saving my mony for it. It has a big fat tale and lite blue legs. It is only 4 inces and is $40.00. We are going to caviwins on thevsday and we are going to the beache on Satrday. I was so happy to see you. Insted of bats in my bat house they are in the atick.

Love
Parker

real size

Don's wife Joyce died in 2002 after they had been married nearly fifty years. They had six children and ten grandchildren. In 2005 Don married Judith Freund Pilgrim, who brought four children and three grandchildren into the family. In 2007 Macalester College awarded Beisswenger an honorary doctor of humane letters degree.

Remarks from Prisoners

Rarely do academicians become prisoners. Even more rarely do prisoners find the gifts of confinement, for those gifts are revealed only to those who embrace their own incarceration. Don is one of the rarities, and he uses his voice to say that which so many other prisoners cannot.

—AL HUGHES
Riverbend Maximum Security Institution
Nashville, Tennessee

In the 1970s persons like the Berrigans [Daniel and Philip] described how the prison system wounds the human spirit. Don Beisswenger continues the same sage perspective of prison life, revealing his own struggle to keep his spirit alive. In six months he captured the essence of how the wounding process occurs and the struggle [of prisoners] to maintain a vital life.

—THOMAS WARREN
Riverbend Maximum Security Institution

I am a prisoner because I committed a crime that did incredible harm to my victims. Don Beisswenger committed a crime that was designed to prevent incredible harm to the oppressed by American-trained terrorists. What is sad is that he was treated the same way I am treated.

—ED MCKEOWN
Riverbend Maximum Security Institution

More Praise for *Locked Up*

We live in a season ripe with the need and opportunity for Christian witness through nonviolent resistance. Don Beisswenger has not only dramatized the cost of speaking truth to power but also has provided a day-by-day description of life as an inmate in federal prison. One can only be grateful for this story and its challenge to each of us to find our own bold expression of God's justice in a world crowded with idols.

—REV. BILL BARNES
Former pastor (1966–1996), Edgehill United Methodist Church
Nashville, Tennessee

Locked Up offers a brief but profound glimpse into a contemporary soul intent on following his Christ with little regard for the cost. Don Beisswenger's memoir reveals a simple humanity that gently prods those of us who are timid about expressing our faith. Reading it gives us hope that we too might find a bolder place to stand, and the courage to endure a higher penalty for believing in a better world.

—REV. DAVID KIDD
Pastor, Hillsboro Presbyterian Church
Nashville, Tennessee

In *Locked Up* we have truth telling at a cost, spiritual reflections at the base, and faith and politics from the hellhole of prison. This story is love in action and a major contribution to the peace and justice movement from someone inside the domination system. *Locked Up* is a must read for prisoners and those who ought to be in prison.

—MURPHY DAVIS, Southern Prison Ministry
BROTHER EDUARD-THE-AGITATOR LORING, Open Door Community
Atlanta, Georgia